I0210743

Author's sketch made from a photograph taken of the *Sultana* on April 26, 1865, at Helena, Arkansas.

THE SULTANA SAGA

THE TITANIC
OF THE
MISSISSIPPI

Rex T. Jackson

HERITAGE BOOKS
2010

HERITAGE BOOKS
AN IMPRINT OF HERITAGE BOOKS, INC.

Books, CDs, and more—Worldwide

For our listing of thousands of titles see our website
at
www.HeritageBooks.com

Published 2010 by
HERITAGE BOOKS, INC.
Publishing Division
100 Railroad Ave. #104
Westminster, Maryland 21157

International Standard Book Numbers
Paperbound: 978-0-7884-2358-1
Clothbound: 978-0-7884-8343-1

The
Sultana Saga
The Titanic
of the Mississippi

Rex T. Jackson

Dedicated to my father
Ernest Jacob Jackson
1922-1998
And
To all the passengers of the
Ill-fated Sultana

Contents

Preface

Those who survived the carnage and bloodshed of the Civil War were men who demonstrated courage and valor under fire, as they faced a blazing din of lead on the many battlefields east and west of the Mississippi River. There were others, after having endured the horrors of fierce battle, who were taken prisoner, experiencing disease, starvation, and all manner of human suffering in prison camps until the war's end.

However, few could conceive that many of these same brave souls, after having suffered through such trials and tribulations as these, would find themselves finally headed home aboard a doomed, overloaded riverboat steamer and have to struggle for their lives in the cold swift currents of the Mississippi River and witness the demise of hundreds of their comrades in arms - after the war was over and peace was declared.

Rex T. Jackson

Edited by: Dr. Fred Pfister
Of **The Ozarks Mountaineer** magazine

.

The Sultana Saga:

The Titanic Of the Mississippi

Chapter 1

Perilous Waters

The perils of the sea have often times proved to be unforgiving, and have claimed the souls of many who have dared to make it their challenge. Throughout history, the deep blue has taken down to its depth a host of man's greatest technological achievements built to master it. These grand ships and boats made by the hand of man, which failed their appointed tasks, are commonly thought to have met their demise on the vast deep oceans of the world; but it may come as a revelation to some, that the worst of all these terrible disasters happened not on the high seas but on the Mississippi River in the heart of America - coming at the most inopportune time to the most undeserving victims.

When travel between America and Europe spawned the need for a means to transport a larger number of passengers, the British Cunard Line, founded in 1839, introduced a transatlantic ship called the *Britannia,* which set off on its maiden voyage July 4, 1840. The ship could carry 115 passengers from Liverpool to Halifax in 12 days and 10 hours.[1]

In a quest for the largest most luxurious of all seafaring liners, the White Star Line, founded in 1845 at Liverpool, began construction of two new ships - the *Olympic* and *Titanic*. Harland and Wolff was authorized to do the work at their Belfast shipyard on April 30, 1907. The *RMS Titanic,* at 46,000-tons, was billed as "practically unsinkable," because of its sixteen watertight compartments, and was launched May 31, 1911. Fully loaded, this massive majestic ship measuring 882 ft. 9 in. in length, with a beam 92 ft. 6 in. and a draught of 34 ft., was certified to carry a total of 3,300 passengers and crew.[2]

On the night of April 14, 1912, Frederick Fleet, the lookout in the crow's nest, spotting danger ahead, rang the 16 in. brass bell and called the bridge, saying: "Iceberg Right Ahead!" The *Titanic's* fate was sealed on its maiden voyage, where no fewer than 1,513 souls perished in the icy waters of the Atlantic out of the more than 2,220 passengers and crew aboard.[3]

Washington Dodge, a survivor of the disaster, spoke about that dreadful night at sea, and said: "The liner was struck on the starboard side, near the bow. The bow, it seemed, withstood the crash, but water rushed into several compartments at the same time. There was complete order among the passengers and crew. We really didn't think there was any danger. We were assured that the ship would float and that there were plenty vessels in reach of wireless to come to our aid if that should become necessary. Then the sinking of the Titanic by the head began and the crew was ordered to man the boats."[4]

Another passenger, Mrs. Churchill Candee, who witnessed the sight, had this to report of that night to remember: "The ice pack which we encountered was fifty-six miles long, I have since heard. When we collided with the mountainous mass it was nearly midnight Sunday. There were two distinct shocks, each shaking the ship violently, but fear did not spread among the passengers immediately. They seemed not to realize what had happened, but the captain and other officers did not endeavor to minimize the danger. The first thing I recall was one of the crew appearing with pieces of ice in his hands. He said he had gathered them from the bow of the boat. Some of the passengers were inclined to believe he was joking. But soon the situation dawned on all of us. The lifeboats were ordered lowered and manned and the word went around that women and children were to be taken off first...The ship settled slowly, the lights going out deck after deck as water reached them. The final plunge, however, was sudden and accompanied by explosions, the effect of which was a horrible sight. Victims standing on the upper deck toward the stern were hurled into the air and fell into the treacherous ice-covered sea. Some were rescued, but most of them perished."[5]

According to Mrs. John M. Brown, the experience of the *Titanic* was the "most harrowing and terrible that any living soul could undergo." While she looked on helplessly, Mrs. Brown said that she "saw the huge liner split in half, with a pang almost as keen as if I had seen somebody die. The following horrors have never left me, day or night. I saw dead bodies of brave men float past the lifeboats. I heard the death cries of women and saw the terrible desolation of the wreck by dawn."[6]

Another survivor recalled that the *Titanic* looked like "a fairytale picture illuminated from stem to stern. Then suddenly the lights began to go out and the stern reared up high in the air. An immense clamor rose on all sides, and during an hour anguished cries rang out. It was like a great chorus chanting a refrain to death with wild obstinacy. Sometimes the cries died out and then the tragic chorus again more terribly and more despairingly. Those shrieks pursued us and haunted us as we pulled away in the night. Then one by one the cries ceased, and only the noise of the sea remained. The Titanic was engulfed almost without a murmur. Her stern quivered in a final spasm and then disappeared."[7]

Lady Duff-Gordon, while floating nearby in one of the lifeboats, also lived to tell the tale of what she experienced firsthand that sad historic chilling night on the cold calm Atlantic, saying: "Then there was another great explosion and the great stern of the Titanic sank as though a great hand was pushing it gently down under the waves. As it went, the screaming of the poor souls left on board seemed to grow louder. It took the Titanic but a short time to sink after that last explosion. It went down slowly without a ripple. We had heard the danger of suction when one of these great liners sink. There was no such thing about the sinking of the Titanic. The amazing part of it all to me as I sat there in the boat, looking at this monster being, was that it all could be accomplished so gently. Then began the real agonies of the night. Up to that time no one in our boat, and I imagine no one in any of the other boats, had really thought that the Titanic was going to sink. For a moment a silence seemed to hang over everything, and then from the water about where the Titanic had been arose bedlam of shrieks and cries. There were women and men clinging to the bits of wreckage in the icy water. It was at least an hour before the last shrieks died out. I remember next the very last cry was that of a man who had been calling loudly: 'My God! My God!' He cried monotonously, in a dull, hopeless way. For an entire hour there had been an awful chorus of shrieks gradually dying into a hopeless moan until this last cry that I spoke of. Then all was silent. When the awful silence came we waited gloomily in the boats throughout the rest of the night."[8]

The *Titanic* has not been the only sinking of such magnitude; in May of 1914, the Canadian Pacific Railway's *RMS Impress of Ireland,* with 1,477 on board, was on the St. Lawrence River heading toward the Atlantic Ocean near Rimouski, Quebec. It succumbed to a watery grave in just 14 minutes, after it was hit in the dense fog by the *Storstad,* a Norwegian ship. Out of the total number aboard, 1,012 persons were lost; which included 159 children.[9]

During World War I, the *Lusitania,* believed to be carrying arms for the Allied efforts, was sunk by a torpedo without warning by a German U-boat on May 7, 1915, off the coast of southern Ireland. The Cunard liner could carry 560 in first class accommodations, 475 in second class and 1,300 in third class. It sank in less than twenty minutes and took the lives of 1,198 along with it.[10]

The rivers of America became crowded during the steamboat era and they also had their share of disasters such as the boiler explosion of the steamboat *Saluda* on April 9, 1852, near Lexington, Missouri, on the Missouri River. More than 100, by some accounts, lost their lives when they were suddenly and violently blown into the river. The victims were said to have been mostly Mormon converts en route to Salt Lake City from Great Britain.[11]

As for the poor souls aboard the *Saluda,* the horror of the blast was graphically described by a local journalist of Lexington: "The mangled remains of human beings were scattered over the wharf and on the bluff; and human blood, just warm from the heart, trickled down the banks and mingled with the water of the Missouri."[12]

Mark Twain tells in his book *Life on the Mississippi* about the awful catastrophe of the steamer *Pennsylvania* which exploded on the Mississippi River, near Ship Island, June 13, 1858, about sixty miles below Memphis, Tennessee. The thunderous crash claimed the life of his dear brother Henry, among others, as "the whole forward third of the boat was hoisted toward the sky!"[13]

According to the *Missouri Republican,* June 16, 1858, it read: "The steamer Pennsylvania left New Orleans on the 9th, with one hundred and twenty-five cabin passengers and one hundred and fifty-eight deckers. She afterwards took on board, at Baton Rouge, Nathez and Vicksburg, 62 passengers, and at Napoleon 10. There were 40 deck hands and fireman; 24 of the steward's crew, and 16 officers - making in all 450 souls. Out of this number, 182 were rescued by a wood boat, and about 70 others escaped in various ways. These numbers include the wounded and scalded. About 200 are lost and missing."[14]

There have been many terrible and deadly historical events which happened on perilous waters, but none more tragic than the sinking of the *Sultana;* the greatest single maritime disaster in U.S. history - the *Titanic* of the Mississippi.

Chapter 2

Long Hard Journey

The way home became a long and winding road for every man who fought in the Civil War. What they would experience along the way, and on the many battlefields, would testify to the resilience of the human spirit. Thousands of these men bravely perished for their faith, while visions of home pulled and tugged at their homesick souls. Through walls of fiery metal and crashes of musketry, the strength and endurance of these soldiers was forged; here they learned not the romance, but all the realities of war.

The path to the *Sultana,* for its passengers, would be paved in blood that measured and marked out the boundaries of hallowed ground in steady streams of lead rifle and cannon balls. The insatiated butchery of those battlefields, would become the first trials and tribulations of their long hard journey to the Mississippi.

8 TITANIC OF THE MISSISSIPPI

On April 12, 1861, a circle of five Confederate batteries commanded by General Pierre Gustave T. Beauregard, of Louisiana, under orders from Confederate President Jefferson Davis to demand evacuation of Fort Sumter off Charleston harbor, South Carolina, opened fire on its thick brick walls. The lonely soldiers inside the fort, waiting for a relief expedition to arrive, were commanded by Major Robert Anderson, a loyal Virginian. For about forty hours the small garrison of eighty-three men bravely held out against the bombardment of the big seacoast guns and mortars until, finally, Major Anderson and his exhausted men surrendered from a bloodless battle, blackened by smoke and cinders. Sunday afternoon, April 14, 1861, with the fort ablaze, the stars and bars of the flag of the Confederate States of America replaced the flag of the Union over Fort Sumter - the Civil War had officially begun.[1]

The military operation would be fought in two primary stags - an eastern and western theater of war that was bound in by the Missouri, Ohio, and Potomac rivers to the north, and by the states of Texas, Arkansas, and Missouri, in the west. According to Federal strategy, their armies were to move toward Richmond, Virginia (the Confederate capital), while protecting their own capital of Washington, in the eastern theater; and in the west, seize control of the Mississippi River to navigate southward with men and supplies then, northward through Georgia, the Carolinas, and finally, on to Richmond.[2]

With Washington and Richmond only about one hundred miles apart, Virginia became a major battleground during the War of the States. On July 16, 1861, Union troops under General Irwin McDowell moved toward Manassas Junction. With many believing that the "rebels" would be easily beaten and Richmond quickly captured, Congressmen and citizens of nearby Washington turned out in force to view the unfolding spectacle. On the other side of the waters of Bull Run though, lay Beauregard's southern troops. During the five hour battle which followed, General Barnard Bee of South Carolina rallied his broken brigade and was reported saying about Thomas J. Jackson: "There is Jackson standing like a stone wall! Rally behind the Virginians!" Jackson and his men, standing firm, had earned the names "Stonewall" Jackson and the "Stonewall Brigade."[3]

The 1st Battle of Manassas (or Bull Run according to the Northerners), was a victory for the South, as Union soldiers, and those of Washington society who had come to see the sight, became panic-stricken and ran for their lives; but not before they had witnessed the death of many brave soldiers.[4] It would only be the beginning of the type of things that the men who were to board the *Sultana* would experience. There would be many bloody battles during those long years of the Civil War, and the brave men of the doomed *Sultana* would be there to fight in many of them.

John D. Imboden, Brigadier General, C.S.A., tells of the hardships he witnessed in retreat from Gettysburg: "The column moved rapidly, considering the rough roads and the darkness, and from almost every wagon for many miles issued heart-rending wails of agony. For four hours I hurried forward on my way to the front, and in all that time I was never out of hearing of the groans and cries of the wounded and dying. Scarcely one in a hundred had received adequate surgical aid, owing to the demands on the hard-working surgeons from still worse cases that had to be left behind. Many of the wounded in the wagons had been without food for thirty-six hours. Their torn and bloody clothing, matted and hardened, was rasping the tender, inflamed, and still oozing wounds. Very few of the wagons had even a layer of straw in them, and all were without springs. The road was rough and rocky from the heavy washings of the preceding day. The jolting was enough to have killed strong men, if long exposed to it. From nearly every wagon as the teams trotted on, urged by whip and shout, came such cries and shrieks as these: 'O God! why can't I die?' 'My

God! will no one have mercy and kill me?' 'Stop! Oh! For God's sake, stop just for one minute; take me out and leave me to die on the roadside.' 'I am dying! My poor wife, my dear children, what will become of you?' Some were simply moaning; some were praying, and others uttering the most fearful oaths and execrations that despair and agony could wring from them...During this one night I realized more of the horrors of war than I had in all the two preceding years."[5]

Writing about hunger, George Cary Eggleston, of Lamkin's Virginia Battery, learned at Cold Harbor its unforgettable truth: "But what is the use of writing about the pangs of hunger? The words are utterly meaningless to persons who have never known actual starvation, and cannot be made otherwise than meaningless...It is a great despairing cry of a wasting body - a cry of flesh and blood, marrow, nerves, bones, and faculties for strength with which to exist and to endure existence. It is a horror which, once suffered, leaves an impression that is never erased from the memory...."[6]

In order to get coffee, sugar, and other such luxuries, soldiers would rob the haversacks of the dead. E.M. Law recalled what his hungry Confederate comrades would do to obtain these things: "It is astonishing into what close places a hungry Confederate would go to get something to eat. Men would sometimes go out under a severe fire, in the hope of finding a full haversack."[7]

Franc B. Wilkie, in his book *Pen and Powder,* attempts to describe the hardships at Fort Donelson: "How the men on both sides fought in the ravines, over the bluffs, amid the dense undergrowth, the jagged rocks, and *abatis;* how they fell wounded, dead; how they advanced and retreated; and how the tides of carnage ebbed and flowed, - I need not tell. All these are matters of history. That night the weather became cold and the streams were frozen and a light snow began to fall toward morning. There were no tents nor fires, and the troops suffered intensely; if the uninjured found the cold unendurable, what must have been the condition of the wounded? Hundreds of them lay out all this dreary night, without shelter, food, water, or medical attendance. Many died who, amid other surroundings, would have recovered. It was horrible beyond comprehension, and yet without remedy."[8]

The terrible slaughter at the battle of Shiloh left the nation astounded by the loss of over 20,000 souls, to which, General Grant, had this to say: "I saw an open field in our possession the second day, over which the Confederates had made repeated charges the day before, so covered with dead that it would have been possible to walk across the clearing, in any direction, stepping on dead bodies, without touching the ground...."[9]

The losses at Spotsylvania were so terrible after the armies had battled for hours, that the place became known as the "Bloody Angle." Charles A. Dana recalled that the "night was coming on, and, after the horrible din of the day, the silence was intense; nothing broke it but distant and occasional firing or the low groans of the wounded. I remember that as I stood there I was almost startled to hear a bird twittering in a tree...The ground was thick with dead and wounded men, among whom the relief corps was at work. The earth, which was soft from the heavy rains we had been having before and during the battle, had been trampled by the fighting of the thousands of men until it was soft, like thin hasty pudding...As we stood there, looking silently down at it, of a sudden the leg of a man was lifted up from the pool and the mud dripped off his boot. It was so unexpected, so horrible, that for a moment we were stunned. Then we pulled ourselves together and called to some soldiers near by to rescue the owner of the leg. They pulled him out with but little trouble, and discovered that he was not dead, only wounded...."[10]

One soldier remembered how horrible it was hunting for the dead and wounded by night: "Nothing could be more dismal and appalling than searching over a battlefield in a dark night for a friend or comrade. To turn up one dead cold face after another to the glimmering light of a lantern, and see it marred with wounds and disfigured with blood and soil, the features, perhaps, convulsed by the death-agony, the eyes vacant and staring, - surely that friendship must be, indeed, stronger than death which would prompt to such an office, yet it was often undertaken, and even by women! Dismal, too, the sight of the dark battle-ground, with lanterns twinkling here and there, 'like the wisp on the morass!'"[11]

A Union officer had this to say about the effects of grapeshot and canister the day after the Battle of Malvern Hill: "...the level rays of the morning sun from our right were just penetrating the fog, and slowly lifting its [lingering] shreds and yellow masses. Our ears had been filled with agonizing cries from thousands before the fog was lifted, but now our eyes saw an appalling spectacle upon the slopes down to the woodlands half a mile away. Over five thousand dead and wounded men were on the ground, in every attitude of distress. A third of them were dead or dying, but enough of them were alive and moving to give to the field a singular crawling effect."[12]

The scenes after the Battle of Antietam were no less appalling, especially those on the "sunken road," according to Charles Coffin he "went past the Roulette's house to the sunken road. The hillside was dotted with prostrate forms of men in blue, but in the sunken road, what a ghastly spectacle! The Confederates had gone down as the grass falls before the scythe. Words are inadequate to portray the scene."[13]

While making an inspection in and around the Malvern house of the condition of his men, Major General Fitz John Porter made this observation: "On the occasion of this visit we frequently witnessed scenes which would melt the stoutest heart...We saw the amputated limbs and the bodies of the dead hurried out of the room for burial. On every side we heard the appeals of the unattended, the moans of the dying, and the shrieks of those under the knife of the surgeon. We gave what cheer we could, and left with heavy hearts."[14]

About war, only eyewitnesses and those who have participated can truly fathom the gravity of actual combat or a soldier's life in the field. Many of the ex-soldiers of war who were to be transported home on the decks of the doomed *Sultana* side-wheeler, incredibly, endured even more - the infamous Andersonville and Cahaba prison camps.

Chapter 3

Hellholes of War

Even before the volleys of musket-fire and the booming of cannons had ceased, thousands of battle-hardened soldiers had already been captured and taken prisoner. The terrible and untold horrors of fierce fighting they endured would not compare to the gruesome inhumanity of their captivity in Civil War prison camps.

Steamers and train cars transported crowded loads of human cargo to the fate of these dark and gloomy walls of confinement where there awaited the grim reaper of vermin, starvation, disease, exposure, and, finally death. The dreadful existence of prison life was such that a soldier's chance of surviving a storm of shot and shell on a field of fierce battle was greater than the hope of these gaunt men surviving incarceration. The gangplank of the *Sultana*, and the comforts of home and family, was but a pipe dream to the inmates of these hellholes of the Civil War.

One of the most well-known of all such camps, where many of the *Sultana's* passengers were held, was the Andersonville prison of the Confederacy, which began in January, 1864, near Americus, Georgia. When constructing the stockade, slaves from local farms were put to the task felling trees on site and digging trenches to set a vertical wall of hand-hewn logs about 20 feet in height. Another wooden fence about 16 to 12 feet high ran within the main stockade. Any prisoner caught within what was called the "deadline" was shot.[1]

The 20 acre site was guarded by rifle pits and artillery emplacements, where as many as 32,899 prisoners were kept safely within the stockade enclosure. Here veterans of many battles of the Civil War, like Stones River, Franklin, Missionary Ridge, Chickamauga and Gettysburg, waited for their freedom. For many of these brave men, their wait ended, never seeing their day of liberation; about 26,436 Confederate soldiers died in various prison camps in the north during the Civil War; while in the south, about 22,576 Union soldiers perished - almost 13,000 of these died while at the Andersonville prison.[2]

On August 5, 1864, Colonel D.T. Chandler, Inspector General, C.S.A., made a disturbing report about conditions at Andersonville, and said: "The acreage gives somewhat less than six square feet to each prisoner (that is, 2 feet by 3). Many (bodies) are carted out daily...whom the medical officers have not seen...The dead are hauled out daily by waggon loads and buried without coffins. Their hands in many instances being mutilated with an axe in removal of any finger rings they may have. It is impossible to state the number of sick, many dying whom the medical officers neither see nor hear of until the remains are brought out for burial."[3]

Speaking from personal experiences, General T. Seymour wrote on August 10, 1864: "At Andersonville, the scene would disgrace a race of cannibal barbarians. Scores die daily from sheer neglect and with less care than a rotten sheep would receive from a brutal owner...I have written fully for the benefit of the thousands who will starve and die in Southern bondage."[4]

More sad appalling observations were made by Dr. Joseph Jones, of the Medical Department, C.S.A., after a visit to Andersonville: "I visited two thousand sick within the stockade lying under some long sheds...At this time only one medical officer was in attendance, whereas at least twenty should have been employed...The sick lay upon bare boards or upon such ragged blankets as they possessed without...any bedding or even straw. The haggard distressed countenances of those miserable, complaining, dejected, living skeletons, crying for medical aid and food...and the ghastly corpses, with their glazed eyeballs staring up into vacant space, with flies swarming down their open and grinning mouths and all over their rugged clothes, infested with numerous lice, as they lay amongst the sick and dying, formed a picture of helpless, hopeless, misery which it would be impossible to portray by words or by the brush. Millions of flies swarmed over everything and covered the faces of the sleeping patients and crawled down their open mouths and deposited their maggots in the gangrenous wounds of the living...Where hospital gangrene was prevailing it was impossible for any wound to escape contagion under these circumstances."[5]

Many Civil War prisoners, with such rate of death around them, "often found themselves wondering and speculating when and how his turn would come; for that it must come, and that soon, seemed inevitable under the circumstances. No words can express the terrible sufferings which hunger and exposure inflicted upon the luckless inmates of Andersonville Prison."[6]

The hot and sultry summer weather took a heavy toll on many, and life in prison became an unimaginable stockade of despair and death: "During July one could scarcely step without seeing some poor victim in his last agonies. The piteous tones of entreaty, the famine-stricken look of these men, their bones in some cases worn through their flesh, were enough to excite pity and compassion in hearts of stone."[7]

These putrid conditions, crowded, and at the mercy of the elements, became a breeding ground for pestilence. In *The Soldier's Story* by Warren Lee Goss, he explains how these problems made it difficult to even breath: "There was a portion of the camp, forming a kind of swamp, on the north side of the branch, as it was termed by the rebels, which ran through the centre of the camp. This swamp was used as a sink by the prisoners, and was putrid with the corruption of human offal. The stench polluted and pervaded the whole atmosphere of the prison. When the prisoner was fortunate enough to get a breath of air outside the prison, it seemed like a new development of creation, so different was it from the poisonous vapors inhaled from the cesspool with which the prison air was reeking. During the day the sun drank up the most noxious of these vapors, but in the night the terrible miasma and stench pervaded the atmosphere to suffocation."[8]

Physically, the men of Andersonville faced death each day they were incarcerated there. Thousands were afflicted with scurvy, for lack of vegetables or wholesome nutritional foods; so that "their limbs were ready to drop from their bodies." By one account, having "seen maggots scooped out by the handful from the scores of those thus afflicted." And again, having "seen forty or fifty men in a dying condition, who, with their little remaining strength, had dragged themselves to this place [the sink] for its convenience, and, unable to get back again, were exposed in the sun, often without food, until death relieved them of the burden of life. Frequently, on passing them, some were found reduced to idiocy, and many, unable to articulate, would stretch forth their wasted hands in piteous supplication for food or water, or point to their lips, their glazed eyes presenting that staring fixedness which immediately precedes death. On some the flesh would be dropping from their bones with scurvy; in others little of humanity remained in their wasted forms but skin drawn over bones. Nothing ever before seen in a civilized country could give one an adequate idea of the physical condition to which disease, starvation, and exposure reduced these men. It was only strange that men should retain life so long as to be reduced to the skeleton condition of the great mass who died in prison."[9]

While the grim reaper appeared and mercifully took scores of souls to realms beyond this horrible place of suffering, those who survived had to adapt mentally "to the circumstances which threaten to crowd him out of existence, or die. He must look upon filth, dirt, innumerable vermin, and even death, with complacency, and not distress himself about that which is unavoidable, while he must never cease battling against them."[10]

Death tolls at Andersonville were 29 percent. The largest prison in the north during the Civil War was Point Lookout in southern Maryland, which had about 20,000 men at one time. The highest death rate in a northern prison camp was 24 percent at Elmira, New York.[11]

Many of the *Sultana's* passengers also came by way of the Cahaba Federal Prison (or unofficially known as Castle Morgan), which was located on the banks of the Alabama and Cahaba rivers near the town of Selma, Alabama. Castle Morgan was first built as a warehouse for cotton and corn - the shed measured about 193 feet by 116 feet, with walls 8 to 10-feet high; it became a prison around June of 1863. It was partially covered by a leaky roof and held between 3,000 to 5,000 inmates. The proximity of the prison to the rivers would allow high waters, due to heavy rain, to flood the camp up to about four feet deep; many prisoners were forced to stand waist deep in the cold swollen river water.[12]

The water supply for the prison left much to be desired according to the Chief Surgeon of the camp: "The supply of water for drinking, cooking, and bathing, as well as for washing, is conveyed from an artesian well, along an open street gutter for 200 yards, thence under the street into the prison. In its course it is subjected to the washings of the hands, feet, faces and heads of soldiers, citizens, and Negroes; in it are rinsed buckets, tubs, and spittoons of groceries, offices, and hospital; in it can be found the filth of hogs, dogs, cows, and horses, and filth of all kinds from the streets and other sources."[13]

James Thomas Wolverton, Co. G, Sixth Tennessee Cavalry, a survivor of the *Sultana,* tells of the rations of corn pone that the prisoners would be issued each day at the Cahaba Federal Prison - that he stowed under his bed for safe keeping, he explains: "The next morning I found that mice had hollowed out a small round hole into the pone and a mother mouse had six little pink babies in it. I just cut out the place and proceeded to eat the rest of the pone. My hunger came first, it had to be appeased."[14]

By the end of the Civil War its death toll was staggering - a total of about 633,000 northern and southern soldiers had died in battle and in prison.[15] In the days to come there would be even more death. Many of the poor souls who lasted long enough for a planned exchange of prisoners were taken by train, steamboat, or on foot, to be held at Camp Fisk; a parole camp four miles from Vicksburg, Mississippi; many, due to their wretched health, died along the way. Then, by April 9, 1865, in a small Virginia town called Appomattox, Grant and Lee would gather together in a farmhouse near the Appomattox Courthouse, Virginia, to draft documents that would bring an end to the madness - the Civil War was over.

The incredible journey, and on the battlegrounds, had forged within its participants a type of strength and endurance to suffering and death never before so profound; and for yet others, being taken captive and transported to the horrors of prison camps, their experience must have surely been such a one which no man should ever have to witness again. But for these men, yet one last titanic event lurked before them, which would steal away their grand jubilation forever.

Chapter 4

Headlines

The month of April, 1865, was a busy one for the newspaper industry and their headlines. With the surrender of Confederate General Lee, the joyful end of the Civil War, the shocking assassination of President Lincoln, and the escape and death of Lincoln's assassin John Wilkes Booth, many papers lacked a respectable response when covering the inconceivable breaking news story that the steamboat *Sultana* had exploded on the Mississippi River and caused a great loss of life.

Readers learned instead that, General Robert E. Lee, when considering surrender, sent one of his staff officers, Lieutenant Colonel Charles Marshall, to find a suitable place for his meeting with General Ulysses S. Grant. Marshall encountered a citizen on the road by the name of Wilmer McLean and inquired of him concerning an appropriate building that would be suitable for the meeting. McLean showed him an empty house which Marshall deemed unfit. Then, McLean offered up his own house - a brick Georgian-style home with a grand piazza that graced the front. It was here, in the McLean House, near the Appomattox Court House, Virginia, on April 9, 1865, that the War Between the States came to a close and brought tears of joy to a war-weary nation hearing the long awaited news.[1]

The jubilation over the war's end would soon be mixed with unbelief and great sorrow in the days to come. On Good Friday, April 14, 1865, President Abraham Lincoln and his wife Mary were attending a popular play, a British comic melodrama by Tom Taylor, *Our American Cousin,* at the Ford's Theatre in Washington, a few blocks east of the White House. Also at the theatre that night was an American actor and violent partisan of the Southern cause, John Wilkes Booth. Booth was born in Bel Air, Maryland, and from 1860 to 1863, he had become known as a successful stage actor in Shakespearean roles. Having played several times at Ford's Theatre he was familiar with the exits and entrances of the playhouse. At about 10:30 p.m., Booth, taking the opportunity when all attention was fixed on the stage, during the second scene of the third act, made his way into the presidential box and put a small pistol to Lincoln's head, between the left ear and the spine, and discharged the weapon. The President was mortally wounded and fell slumped in his rocking chair, unconscious. While a plume of blue and gray smoke hung in box 7, Booth, leaped down to the stage below while shouting the Virginia state motto *"Sic semper Tyrannis,"* which means "Thus ever to tyrants," and, with a broken leg, due to the fall, managed to somehow escape from the theatre and the scene of the crime. His fiendish work would not go unpunished; 12 days later, on April 26, papers would proclaim that justice prevailed, as he was overtaken at a barn near Bowling Green, Virginia, by a platoon of New York Cavalry and killed while resisting arrest.[2]

As for the Chief Executive, he was taken to a lodging house across the street from the Ford's Theatre, which was owned by William Petersen, a tailor, and placed in a bed in a back room on the first floor. At his bedside, keeping a vigil, was his wife, his son Robert, and several Cabinet members who waited throughout the night while surgeons and physicians fought a losing battle to save Lincoln's fading life. At 7:20 a.m., on Saturday, April 15, 1865, the Sixteenth President of the United States of America, Abraham Lincoln, died. As they pulled a sheet over his face, a lament-stricken Secretary of War Edwin M. Stanton, said: "Now he belongs to the ages."[3]

Charles A. Dana, a former managing editor of the *New York Tribune,* was the assistant secretary of war to Stanton, and in his book *Recollections of the Civil War,* he remembered that tragic time that shocked the nation: "That night I was awakened from a sound sleep by a messenger with the news that Mr. Lincoln had been shot, and that the Secretary wanted me in a house in Tenth Street. I found the President with a bullet wound in the head, lying unconscious, though breathing heavily, on a bed in a small side room, while all the members of the Cabinet, and the Chief Justice with them, were gathered in the adjoining parlor. They seemed to be almost as much paralyzed as the unconscious sufferer within the little chamber. The surgeons said there was no hope. Mr. Stanton alone was in full activity."[4]

The business of keeping the Government in order, despite the grievous drama at hand, left Secretary Stanton to say to his assistant Dana, "Sit down here, I want you." Stanton then, at that time, according to Dana, "began and dictated orders, one after another, which I wrote out and sent swiftly to the telegraph. All these orders were designed to keep the business of the Government in full motion until the crisis should be over. It seemed as if Mr. Stanton thought of everything, and there was a great deal to be thought of that night. The extent of the conspiracy was, of course, unknown, and the horrible beginning which had been made naturally led us to suspect the worst. The safety of Washington must be looked after. Commanders all over the country had to be ordered to take extra precautions. The people must be notified of the tragedy. The assassins must be captured. The coolness and clearheadedness of Mr. Stanton under these circumstances were most remarkable. I remember that one of his first telegrams was to General Dix, the military commander of New York, notifying him of what had happened. No clearer brief account of the tragedy exists to-day than this, written scarcely three hours after the scene in Ford's Theater, on a little stand in the room where, a few feet away, Mr. Lincoln lay dying."[5]

After his death, Lincoln's body was taken to the East Room of the White House to lay in state. Bells tolled in the streets, as deep and dark lamenting gloom and sadness overwhelmed many citizens. This was a strange contrast to the wide-spread joy that had been expressed since the end of the war had been announced, just a few days before. On April 19, Lincoln received a military funeral in Washington befitting a president; then, on April 21, his coffin was placed on a special train bound for his home state of Springfield, Illinois, where he was buried at the Oak Ridge Cemetery.

The jubilee that followed the end of the war, would only be equaled in comparison by the sorrowful lamentation when the news came of the tragic untimely death of President Lincoln. While a nation in shock struggled to cope with the unthinkable, the ill-fated *Sultana* was already steaming up the Mississippi River on its way to rendezvous with death and disaster, and its headlines destine to be outweighed and overshadowed by the chaos which had preceded it.

The great mighty Mississippi that ran through America's midsection was full of steamboat dangers. Hidden within its currents were tangled masses of sunken timbers, sandbars, or submerged forests which could rip open a hull, leaving many boats and their passengers at the mercy of the river. Those who chose the life of the river enjoyed the luxury the riverboat steamers had to offer regardless of the drift logs or the threat of an exploding boiler. The Mississippi was to become the scene of a crowded way of life in the 1800's.

Chapter 5

The Advent
Of the *Sultana*

Long before there were modern-day roads crisscrossing the American landscape, bustling with automobiles, buses, and diesel powered semi-tractor trailer rigs, meandering rivers served as natural super highways. As time went on, the vessels that were used to ply the rivers improved and became larger and more powerful as the need demanded. The waterways of the 18th and 19th centuries were a lifeline to the growth and further expansion of the nation; on them plied flatboats, steamboats, and various other crafts designed to carry goods and passengers to wharfs and landings along the banks of its many rivers.

The earliest recorded riverboat to apply the use of steam power was in 1786, by an American inventor named John Fitch. As a result of launching his small experimental steamboat on the waters of the Delaware River, he was encouraged, due to its success, to build a second steamer in 1788, that reached the speed of more than 6 miles per hour.[1]

The first successful vessel powered by steam to reach commercial success was the steamboat *Clermont,* called "Fulton's Folly" by those who first witnessed it. The *Clermont,* at 133 feet in length and 18 feet in width, was designed by Robert Fulton, another American inventor, and was launched on August 17, 1807. Its famous run from New York to Albany on the Hudson River resulted in a patent for Fulton and his design. The steamboats that he built in the years that followed would ply the Raritan, Potomac, and Mississippi rivers; he was also responsible for building the *Fulton the First* - the first steam driven warship.[2]

Before long, steam would also be used to traverse the vast distance of the Atlantic Ocean between America and Europe. On May 24, 1819, the converted coastal packet ship *Savannah,* left Savannah, Georgia, and reached Liverpool, England, on June 20, 1819. It wasn't until 1840 that the Cunard Line began regular transatlantic crossings.[3]

On January 3, 1863, two of the largest hulls of their time were launched into the icy waters of the Ohio River at Litherburg Shipyard in Cincinnati: the *Luminary* and the ill-fated *Sultana,* a 260-foot wooden-hulled side wheel riverboat steamer. The *Sultana,* had a 42-foot beam and a hold seven feet deep. The brainchild of Captain Preston Lodwick, the *USS Sultana* was rated at 1,000 tons of capacity and trimmed in only 34 inches of water. Built at a cost of sixty thousand dollars, the elegant steamer was licensed to accommodate seventy-six cabin passengers and three hundred deck passengers and crew. Designed especially with the inland waterways in mind, the *Sultana's* hull was constructed with a flat bottom. The Cincinnati *Daily Commercial* hailed the new riverboat as "one of the largest and best business steamers ever constructed."[4]

There were four cylindrical coal-burning boilers on the

main deck, 18 feet long and 46 inches in diameter. However, the boilers that were installed in the *Sultana* were the new fire-tube type, invented by Randolph Elder of Scotland in 1862, which heated the river-water, not just from the bottom but on the inside, by way of twenty-four five-inch flues in each boiler. The boilers were more efficient, but proved to be dangerous when used on muddy rivers like the lower Mississippi River. The amount of mud in the water, that was taken from the river could build up inside the flues and cause dry areas, which could become super-heated when the flues were denied the water flow that cooled them, resulting in a boiler explosion.[5] The two engines had 25-inch cylinders with eight-foot stokes, which turned two side water-wheels that were thirty-four feet in diameter. Built mainly for the lower Mississippi cotton-trade, the *Sultana,* like a floating palace, had glittering glass chandeliers and ornate Victorian charm, as it steamed gracefully along the Ohio and Tennessee rivers, with regular runs on the Mississippi, between St. Louis, Missouri, and New Orleans, Louisiana.[6]

The highly competitive riverboat business treated passengers aboard such boats as the *Sultana,* to the comforts of small but luxurious staterooms; passengers of the steamboat era could enjoy the scenic countryside from the boiler-deck promenade. Their stately appointments would only later be exceeded by grand seafaring ships.[7]

Lower class blacks and whites were allowed to travel in deck accommodations; much like it was for "steerage" passengers on the great ocean liners of the early nineteen hundreds. Food was served to them on mere tin plates and they were expected to be able to sleep on bare planks; which they endured for this, then, modern convenience of river-travel.[8]

In the early to mid-1800's, the life expectancy of riverboats was only about four or five years, due to snags, debris, collisions, and other perils of river navigation; during that time, however, almost two hundred of these disasters were caused by boiler explosions. The dangers aboard these luxurious river vessels were well-known, yet the allure of their speed and comfortable accommodations superseded the public's fears.[9]

On the morning of April 15, 1865, the *Sultana* left Cairo, Illinois, en route to New Orleans; while it steamed southward, bells tolled the sad astonishing news of the death of President Abraham Lincoln. By April 19, 1865, the *Sultana* had reached New Orleans and brought the word of the assassination of Lincoln along with it. The newspapers of the South were ordered by Secretary of War Stanton not to print anything with regard to the Lincoln assassination, and many disbelieved the facts of the incredible news brought to them by the passengers of the *Sultana*.[10]

Leaving New Orleans on April 21, 1865, the *Sultana* had between 75 to 100 passengers - men, women and children; and a cargo of a hundred hogshead of sugar and a hundred head of various livestock. The trip back up the Mississippi was impeded by the powerful currents caused by the heavy spring rains and snow melt, which placed even more burden on the *Sultana*. About seventy-five miles south of Vicksburg, Mississippi, Nathan Wintringer, the chief engineer, made a disturbing discovery - a boiler was leaking from a bulging seam. After consulting with the captain of the *Sultana*, J.C. Mason, it was decided to reduce speed and make repairs at Vicksburg.[11]

The *Sultana* arrived at Vicksburg on the evening of April 23, 1865, where Wintringer sought out a competent local boilermaker from Klein's Foundry, R. G. Taylor, to effect repairs to the defective boiler. Taylor reported to Captain Mason and Wintringer that two new sheets adjoining the leak needed to be taken out and replaced to insure a thorough and permanent repair. However, his professional advice was ignored and he was persuaded, against his better judgment, to simply apply a twenty-six by eleven-inch patch directly over the bulged area; the patch was one-quarter inch in thickness -

less than the regular boiler plating. The repairs at Vicksburg took over twenty hours to complete.[12]

While all of the repairs were taking place, a local business agent of the *Sultana* brought the news of the prison exchange camp of recently released Federal prisoners from Confederate stockades (Andersonville and Cahaba), that would be available for passage to Cairo on the waiting steamer. Standard price for enlisted men was normally five dollars and ten dollars for officers - a very lucrative opportunity indeed. The first boatload of prisoners, about 1,300, was not taken by the *Sultana* but by the *Henry Ames* the day before on April 22.[13]

Scores of bony dried-up men, walking skeletons, who were exchange prisoners, were now at last free men, as word had finally come that the war was over. They were quickly marched from the holding area at Camp Fisk, which was about four miles from Vicksburg, by Captain George A. Williams of the 1st U.S. Infantry, and crammed aboard the waiting *Sultana*; wretched parolee after parolee, along with dozens of surplus army mules, horses, and hogs, were packed like sardines onto the doomed steamer - filling every nook and cranny of its deck and hold.[14]

The prisoners who were now on the *Sultana* and overjoyed to finally be headed in the direction of home, had no idea what unspeakable fate awaited them upriver; they only knew of the horrible places they had been, and the terrible things they had witnessed. In their excitement, other dangerous possibilities were out-of-mind.

Here they were at last, having faced the awful reality of war, the hornet humming of mini balls, the earsplitting roar of cannons and of iron and laden hail. These brave men were homeward bound away from such things, as was reported by Warren Lee Goss: "...while from their rifle-pits came a hum of bullets and crackle of musketry. Their heavy shot came crashing among the tangled abatis of fallen timber, and plowed up the dirt in our front, rebounding and tearing through the branches of the woods in our rear. The constant hissing of the bullets...whispering around into us, gave me a sickening feeling and cold perspiration. I felt weak around my knees - a sort of faintness and lack of strength in the joints of my legs, as if they would sink from under me. These symptoms did not decrease when several of my comrades were hit. The little rifle-pits in our front fairly blazed with musketry, and the continuous *snap, snap, crack, crack* was murderous."[15]

They were now looking forward to their own livelihoods, and a brighter future with every hope that all such past horrors would be forever behind them. The nightmares that haunted their minds about Andersonville and Cahaba, the sores that afflicted them, starvation, abuse, vermin, disease and all the horrors of prison-life - these things were finally over - they would be headed home and north.

Daniel Garber tells of that moment in time: "We started up the broad Mississippi with fond hopes of soon seeing the dear ones at home, but how few of us had the pleasure of realizing these hopes."[16]

Private James R. Collins, Company F, 3rd Tennessee Cavalry, also spoke about the morale on board the *Sultana* that day: "Many a weary soldier at night in the ill-fated boat dreaming of loved ones, full of inexpressible happiness that at last all dangers and hardships were over, and that the white dove of peace had perched upon the flags of the hostile armies, and songs and laughter would take the place of groans and tears of agony."[17]

Another man, W. C. Porter, tells of the joyous conditions aboard the *Sultana* just prior to the disaster: "...we had a very pleasant ride. All were joyous and happy with the anticipation of seeing home and friends."[18]

According to Samuel H. Raudebaugh, it was a happy time: "...we were on our way home from the cruel war, it being virtually over. We were on our way home from those horrid dens of cruelty and starvation. Yes, we had lived through it all, and hoped, 'Yes, expected soon to see loved ones and home and enjoy at least some of the peace we had fought to restore. Home! Yes, home under the stars and stripes, once more.'"[19]

By the time they left Vicksburg they were about 2,400 strong, the overburdened *Sultana's* big thirty-four foot paddle wheels churned the muddy waters of the Mississippi and labored another thirty hours, or more, until Helena, Arkansas, came into view. It was the morning of April 26, 1865. While there, the only known photograph of the *Sultana* and the poor doomed passengers aboard, was taken by a photographer, amazed at the sight of her crowded decks. When the hoard of men on the steamer realized that they were about to have their picture taken, they suddenly scrambled to the port side railing, which nearly capsized the big outsized riverboat. After about an hour had passed, the *Sultana* once again steamed up river under power.[20]

As the lights of Memphis, Tennessee, loomed ahead, many of the passengers were anxious to go ashore and enjoy some of the simple pleasures they had been denied for so long; luckily for some, they never re-boarded. They had docked there at 6:30 p.m. on April 26, 1865. Passengers disembarked, hogsheads of sugar were unloaded, and once again the leaky troublesome boiler was attended to.[21]

Around midnight, the *Sultana* let loose her mooring lines and cut across-stream to a coal yard on the west bank, in Arkansas. In under an hour, a thousand bushels of coal in burlap bags were carried on board for the trip up the river to Cairo; by able bodied soldiers and roustabouts.[22]

It was 1:00 a.m., April 27, 1865, when the side-wheel riverboat steamer *Sultana* left the Memphis area, heading north, with death and disaster right ahead.[23]

> Poor souls, jubilant and brave
> Midwestern Union soldiers free.
> A grim host upriver awaits, a watery grave;

Fought hard in war, now peacefully.

Unaware of their doom, or fate,
These men sick and frail;
Only minutes before the eternal gate -
From death, still telling their tale.

Chapter 6

Voices
Of the Past

Throughout recorded history, many heart-wrenching events have become common knowledge, but such is not the case of the disaster of the mighty steamer *Sultana*. The drama that unfolded on the Mississippi River in America's heartland received little or no attention by the news media. The first release in the New York *Times*, on April 29, 1865, was only a five-inch item which appeared on page four. The news of the unfortunate affair carried on the longest in the Memphis area, as they were forced to be more involved due to the clean-up and recovery efforts. A piece in the Memphis *Argus*, on May 6, 1865, read: "We have, as a people, become so accustomed to supping up horrors during the past few years that they soon seem to lose their appalling features, and are forgotten. Only a few days ago fifteen hundred lives were sacrificed to fire and water, almost within sight of the city. Yet, even now, the disaster is scarcely mentioned - some new excitement has taken its place."

Somewhere, mingled in the mud and sediment of the great river Mississippi, were left the remains of many victims that were never recovered - forgotten ghosts of pain and torment. The voices of these lost suffering souls, still reverberate, echoing tales from their watery grave of that dark and gloomy ordeal of April 27, 1865. And, even though the circumstances surrounding the loss of the *Sultana* and its many victims would, for some strange unsympathetic reason, cause it to become a mere footnote in American history, it would nevertheless continue to whisper its ghastly experience of this human drama. These voices of the past can still inspire the living and their resounding words of that dreadful never ending night was documented by many eyewitnesses.

On that morning, about seven miles north of Memphis, Tennessee, the *Sultana* carefully made its way through a series of islands called Paddy's Hen and Chicks; and just south of Island Number 41, in a bend in the river, traveling about nine miles per hour, at about 2:00 a.m., suddenly, Taylor's small repair patch on the troubled boiler must have finally gave out. There was a tremendous explosion which reportedly ruptured two of the remaining three boilers in the process. The ensuing blast tore through the decks below and sealed the fate of the *Sultana,* as well as many of its passengers. The explosion was so powerful it was heard back in Memphis.[1]

The explosion of the boilers was so violent that many of the victims were scalded instantly by the superheated steam or were hurled into the air, landing in the cold river. Others were burned or lacerated by flying shrapnel from the burst boilers and debris, while some received broken limbs, or were trapped in the burning and sinking *Sultana.*[2]

Arthur A. Jones, 115th Ohio Volunteer Infantry, attempted to describe the incredible scene: "What a crash! My God! My blood curdles while I write and words are inadequate; no tongue or writer's pen can describe it. Such hissing of steam, the crash of the different decks. As they came together with the tons of living freight, the falling of the massive smoke stacks, the death cry of strong-hearted men caught in every conceivable manner, the red-tongued flames bursting up through the mass of humanity and driving to death's door those who were fortunate enough to live through worse than a dozen deaths in that "damnable deaths pen" at Andersonville. We had faced death day by day while incarcerated there, but this was far more appalling than any scene through which we had passed." He also said that: "Awakened with the dreamy whisper of mother , sister or other darling on our lips. But oh, what a change in one short moment! comrades imploring each other for assistance that they might escape from the burning decks; officers giving orders for the safety of their men; women shrieking for help; horses neighing; mules kicking and making the terrible scene hideous with their awful brays of disaster. These are a few of the many scenes and sounds that greeted my sight and came to my ear."[3]

The horrific blast sent metal fragments of the boilers, machinery parts, and numerable other objects as projectiles through the upper decks, killing and maiming scores of sleeping passengers. Scalding steam attacked the flesh of any it came in contact with.[4]

Many passengers were awakened from the sudden blast, such was the case of James K. Brady, who related his experience this way: "...I was suddenly awakened to the scenes, as the fire was all over me and my friend was trying to brush it off; it had already burned most of the hair off from the top of my head. We finally got the fire out and began looking around for some means of saving ourselves, for we could see that the boat was on fire. We could see nothing to get, so we went to the front of the hurricane deck and took hold of some ropes and went down to the bow of the boat and Oh, what a sight met our gaze! There were some killed in the explosion, lying in the bottom of the boat, being trampled upon, while some were crying and praying, many were cursing while others were singing. That sight I shall never forget; I often see it in my sleep, and wake with a start."[5]

Another witness, George Young, said that: "We found few sound men on the boiler deck, but a large number of injured ones. Some of these were trying to get forward, crawling along with broken limbs or badly scalded, and many implored us for aid, as they could not swim. Some, in their agony, crawled to the edge of the boat and rolled themselves into the water to drown."[6]

With little hope remaining of surviving the burning riverboat steamer, J. Walter Elliott, tells how passengers were made to decide their inevitable fates: "Women and little children in their night clothes, brave men who have stood undaunted on many a battle field, all contribute to the confusion and horror of the scene as they suddenly see the impending death by fire, and wringing their hands, tossing their arms wildly in the air, with cries most heart-rending, they rush pell-mell over the guard into the dark, cold waters of the river."[7]

James Thomas Wolverton, Company G, Sixth Tennessee Cavalry, was one of the few who survived, and had this to say about his experience: "...I felt a terrible shock, followed by a deafening explosion. Before I could think, my head struck water and I went down, down, struggling for breath. Finally, I came to the surface exhausted for breath. I began swimming the best I could with my clothes and shoes on. I grabbed at anything I might get hold on, as I knew it was my only chance. At last, I grasped some pieces of the boat with my left arm, which was hardly sufficient to support me. A little later, some pieces came up between my legs, which helped to keep my head above water."[8]

Another man who lived to tell the tale was William Crisp, 18th Michigan Volunteer Infantry, who, in his own words, adds this: "I was asleep on the Boiller deck about sixteen feet from the Boiler and the great side of the boiler was Blown out and Shut down over me breaking my left shoulder and the heat was intense I seemed to be nailed to the floor. I could not stir hand or foot. I thought I should be roasted alive then and there. I was scalded and burned to death almost when the heat got out some I found I could move and I crawled out of that Hell to the front of the boat and then it was I saw what happened. I could look into the fire and see hundreds of men burning up among the Timbers that Boiler saved me from being crushed to death by the falling timers. Finely the fire drove me into the water and I swam three miles and a half and landed in the trees on the Arkansaw side and I was there until nine oclock in the morning...."[9]

William Fies, a soldier with the 64th Ohio Volunteer Infantry, was there to witness the awful sounding voices of the death throes of his fellowman: "The agonizing shrieks and groans of the injured and dying were heart-rendering, and the stench of burning flesh was intolerable and beyond any power of description...Judging from the injuries I received I must have been knocked senseless by the explosion, as I found the left side of my face bruised and bleeding, my left hand badly scalded, and my left shoulder disabled, which afterwards proved to be a very bad dislocation. When I took in the situation, and saw the dangerous place I was in, I took hold of an iron brace rod near me which was so hot that it actually blistered my hands, and scrambled onto the hurricane deck, where I found a number of men trying to extinguish the fire by throwing water with buckets. From them I first learned that the boilers had exploded. From there I slid down a rope to the bow of the boat, carrying with me a small wooden box, which I thought might become useful to me in case I was compelled to take to the water. I changed my mind, however, and threw it aside. I saw a number of men bringing from the hold empty cracker barrels and jumping overboard with them, but I saw they were worse than useless in keeping the heads of the men above water, having only one head in them they would not balance. Just at this time the stage plank was lowered from its hangings and about as many as could get a hold of it were trying to launch it, first on one side then on the other, finally it went overboard carrying with it a great number, but as it was heavily bound with iron it sank, and must have carried down with it a great many who had hold of it and others who were struggling in the water to keep afloat and save themselves."[10]

"Most of the boys," according to Manly C. White, "stripped off their clothes and jumped into the river, which was cold and swift, and some three or four miles wide, and so dark that you could not see the shore. The scenes were heart-rending; wounded and dying begging for help - some praying, some swearing - while those in the water would catch hold of one another, and go down in squads. The fire was getting so hot that I soon saw that I must get into the water. I was quite an expert swimmer, and thought if I could get away from the crowd I might save myself, though I was quite weak, having been sick a good deal of the time I was in prison. I went to the gangway to go below, but found that it was gone, so I jumped down on the lower deck. What a sight - men dead and dying, parts of bodies, arms, legs, and the wreck of the boat, all in one mangled mass!"[11]

Since the *Sultana* had only one lifeboat, and a limited amount of life belts kept in the staterooms, there was little safety equipment provided on board for the many hundreds in the water (reminiscent of the *Titanic* and some of the problems it would face in the future). The one lifeboat, after it was thrown into the river, soon filled up with panic-stricken passengers who fought their way into it, until it sank below the raging current along with its occupants.[12]

Joseph Taylor Elliott gave this chilling account: "Such screams I never heard - twenty or thirty men jumping off at a time - many lighting on those already in the water - until the river became black with men, their heads bobbing up like corks, and then many disappearing never to appear again. We threw over everything that would float that we could get hold of, for their assistance; and then I, with several others, began tearing the sheets off the sides of the cabin, and throwing it over."[13]

Watching the mass in the water, Sgt. James H. Kimberlin, reported that: "The water around the vessel for a distance of twenty to forty feet was a solid, seething mass of humanity, clinging one to another. The best or luckiest man was on top. I then, after partially dressing, went forward, climbing down the wreckage to the lower deck on the west side, and when I looked out over the water where but a few minutes before there were hundreds of men struggling for supremacy, now there were but few to be seen. The great mass of them had gone down, clinging to each other."[14]

One man swam toward a dark object in the water, which turned out to be a mule that had been blown into the water by the blast. The still-warm beast helped to sustain him until he was rescued three miles below Memphis, still clutching the mule to stay afloat.[15]

Standing along the Tennessee shore, William Wooldridge, was able to see the *Sultana* saga clearly unravel: "Quite a distance out in the river we saw the steamer burning. She seemed a little more than two-thirds the way across - if anything, more toward the Arkansas shore. She was immediately opposite our house. The blaze was shooting far up into the sky when I first saw her. It was so light in our front yard I could have picked up a pin. We could see her timber falling and we heard the cries of hundreds for help. We saw many jumping into the water to save themselves from being burned. We could see them plainly as they struggled in the river. Their cries for help were pitiful. They were indescribable. The impression it made on my mind will never be erased. Finally the burning boat began to resemble a massive ball of fire. It was drifting down river, helpless against a wind and with a strong current back of it."[16]

"I soon realized that a frightful disaster had occurred and heard the groans of the suffering and cries for help," said one survivor, "...Men were shoving off gang planks, some tearing boards off on which to float, others walking through the crowded deck, seemingly crazed or wringing their hands and calling on God for deliverance. Others were crying, while many were being crowded off into the river by dozens and going down to a watery grave clasped in each others embrace. I made my way through the crowd down to the bow of the boat, picking up the hatch door on my way. I dropped it into the water and leaped in after it...as the day dawned on the morning of the 27th of April, 1865, I was picked up by the steamer "Bostonia" and carried to the city of Memphis, Tenn."[17]

The steamboat *Bostonia* was one out of several attempting rescue efforts; arriving, the *Bostonia* lowered its yawl into the Mississippi and began recovering men and women from drifts and debris. The cabin of the *Bostonia* became an emergency hospital and headed back to Memphis with about a hundred souls that were plucked from the water in its temporary care.[18]

By dawn's early morning light, the once grand side wheel steamer *Sultana,* now a fiery furnace of human cremation, slipped under the surface of the mighty Mississippi River just north of Mound City, Arkansas, and disappeared from sight. In a short while, even the smoke and hissing steam gave up its ghost, and fell silent; but the saga was far from over.

So many poor gaunt patriotic souls of war had gone down in death, wanting only to reach their destination, to see friends, family, and loved ones, once more. Struck down, not in fierce battle pierced by lead or bayonet, but by an unforeseen and unexpected circumstance of fate. Taken to eternity, not by the filth of the prison camps from which they came as did so many of their comrades in arms that perished in those camps, but by flames that scalded them, and cold muddy river water that drowned them, when they were unaware of doom.

The rising of the sun in its burst of flaming color, the seasons of spring, summer, fall and winter, the earth in all its glory, forever stolen from these poor wretched souls. They fought, for belief in a better country; they suffered, for the future of generations; they died, with only the hope that these things would come to pass, and that their contribution might help to secure our future liberty.

Chapter 7

Pangs
Of Recovery

In the aftershock of the devastating *Sultana* catastrophe, many would share in the vastness of its outcome, as they would become participants of the gruesome task at hand of search and recovery. For many days and weeks following the ordeal, there were putrid decomposing powerful reminders of what and to whom, this terrible incident of horrific magnitude had struck.

In the light of day, the full impact of the situation became gravely clear, as rescuers beheld the motionless sight of the scores of tortured dead littering the shorelines for miles down river. Like a burial detail assigned to a bloody battleground to deal with the ghastly results of mortal combat, the cleanup of the *Sultana* aftermath was sobering.

The passengers that survived the explosion, the flames, and the cold water, having lived through war, prison camps, and all their trials and tribulations, still would have to go on with the scars and tormenting memories of this eventful night for the rest of their lives - destined to relive the drama again and again as it played out its horrors - sharing their hearts with its many nightmares. There would be many sleepless nights in the years to come.

The Memphis hospital wards worked franticly to save the injured that were being brought to them. They were the Washington, Adams, Gayoso, Overton, Officers, Webster and the Soldier's Home, which treated about 520 victims; about 200 of them could not be saved.[1] In regard to the effort taking place, William Fies later wrote about what he saw: "I was placed in a ward with quite a number who were severely scalded, or otherwise badly injured, and such misery and intense suffering as I witnessed while there is beyond my power to describe. The agonizing cries and groans of the burned and scalded were heartrending and almost unendurable, but in most cases the suffering was of short duration as most of them were relieved by death in a few hours."[2]

While the drama continued on at the Memphis hospitals as a result of the *Sultana*, the rest of the nation grieved the assassination and loss of President Abraham Lincoln, and followed the news of the death of his assassin. The long costly War of the States was at long last over, and the public was in no mood for yet another terrible bloodbath. But in the Memphis *Argus*, its readership read: "Fifteen miles below the city on the east bank of the Mississippi River near the head of Cow Island, the nude and putrefied body of a lady was seen. Hogs were eating the body: Many of the bodies have been picked up in the river by gunboats, wrapped in canvas and thrown overboard."[3]

For weeks bodies were harvested from the river, bloated and disfigured. They appeared in the area of the sunken wreck, and were seen around the cities of Memphis, Fort Pickering and Helena. Riverboats plying the river reported seeing sickening decomposing corpses floating along in the water, washed up on shore or caught in driftwood as far away as Vicksburg. Many were being devoured by hungry hogs and birds.[4]

Phineas D. Parker, an engineer with the steamboat *Vindicator,* explains the problems that dead bodies were causing to steamers on the river: "I wish to say that the most horrible sight I saw during my whole service was immediately after the calamity. When clearing the wheels [the boat's paddle wheels] after the *Sultana* disaster we would find them clogged with dead bodies from the *Sultana.* The crew of the *Vindicator* were mostly old soldiers, and there came very near being a revolt because we were not allowed to bury the bodies which lodged in our wheels."[5]

W.N. Goodrich remembered that on the "morning of the 27th of April boats were coming up the river searching for victims of the disaster. Some of the poor fellows were hanging to the trees, some were on logs, and some were found in almost every conceivable place."[6]

Coming into the wharf at Memphis after being rescued by a boat, Nathan S. Williams, said that: "The sight there was most terrible. The bodies of the dying, wounded and scalded were to be seen on every hand."[7]

The Unites States Custom Department at Memphis made an estimate of the number presumed to have died as a result of the *Sultana* incident, which was 1,547.[8] Another source, *Gould's History of River Navigation,* recorded the number to be 1,647.[9] However, taking into account various reports, and those who died in the hospitals soon after out of the 780 survivors, the death toll would be somewhat higher, around 1,700 to 1,800 souls.[10]

Many of the bodies were never recovered and remained at the mercy of the Mississippi River, and some never surfaced, but were entombed in the *Sultana.* In the Memphis *Daily Bulletin,* May 27, 1865, it read: "The *Sultana* is in 26 feet of water, and settling. On her decks can be seen bones burned to cinders, knives, buttons, spoons, fragments of boots and blankets, and spots on the deck may be seen where the bodies of some victims kept the wood from burning. In a burned and cindered shoe was seen the bones of a foot, and skulls, and blackened limbs were thickly strewn all over. It is a sickening, horrible sight. At low water, the wreck will be high and dry."[11]

Much like the aftermath of the *Sultana,* the *Titanic,* 47 years later, would also have the grim task of painful recovery to perform. In comparing similar disasters, it is easy to see that the *Sultana* is worthy of as much if not more, historical recognition, as other famous wrecks such as the *Titanic.*

After the *Titanic,* the cable ship *Mackay-Bennett* was sent out from Halifax, Nova Scotia, with tons of ice, over 100 coffins, 40 embalmers, and an Anglican cannon for services of sea burials. Its mission in the cold ocean waters of the North Atlantic, was to retrieve deteriorating bodies - men, women and children, from the *Titanic* sinking. On April 20, 1912, the *Mackay-Bennett* recovered fifty-one bodies, one of which was a two-year-old boy.[12]

Several days had passed since the *Titanic* had vanished into the ocean depth, so many of the bodies were so badly decomposed that they were undistinguishable. Those that had property or recognizable features, were embalmed on the *Mackey-Bennett* and returned to Halifax for further identification. Out of the fifty-one, 24 were so disfigured that they were weighed into sacks and given a burial at sea.[13]

Over a period of six weeks, several other ships arrived to aid in the task of recovery. From the waters were plucked another 328 decomposing souls of the *Titanic* disaster. Out of these, a total of 128 were found to be beyond recognition, 119 were buried at sea, while the others were taken to Halifax.[14]

There were services held in the United States, Great Britain and France for the unfortunate victims of the unsinkable ship of dreams, the *Titanic* - pride of the White Star Line. Unlike the *Sultana*, whose name is mostly unheard of, the *Titanic's* name has been resurrected to worldwide fame. When the body of the *Titanic's* bandleader, Wallace Hartley, was returned to his hometown of Colne, Lancashire, people came from near and far to pay homage;[15] while the *Sultana's* victims, who were veterans of war, were unheralded.

Most of the victims of the *Sultana* that were recovered were buried in the Elmwood Cemetery in Memphis. However, in 1867, when the National Military Cemetery was established at Memphis, most of the soldiers were exhumed from Elmwood and reburied at the National Military Cemetery. The majority of the headstones which mark the final resting place of these unfortunate souls, reads: "Unknown U.S. Soldier."[16]

Other such men as these, who have nothing to do with the *Sultana*, are buried with honor in the Arlington National Cemetery on the Federal burial ground, in Arlington County, Virginia, on the Potomac River, across from Washington, D.C. Among the monuments on the grounds is the Tomb of the Unknown Soldier, which exists to represent all the soldiers killed in action who made the supreme sacrifice. Engraved on the tomb is this inscription, that reads: "Here rests in honored glory an American soldier known but to God."

The hundreds of soldiers who perished on the ill-fated *Sultana* were men such as these, just as deserving of honor; serving their country not just in fierce battle, but also as prisoners of war in Andersonville and Cahaba.

Many of survivors went home to face a public who, to their amazement, had heard very little about the disaster. And this, while the heart-wrenching sounds of their fallen comrades still freshly rang out loud and clear, having just experienced it.

Within hours of the disaster an investigation convened to determine the cause of the tragedy. Testimonies were heard by many witnesses pertinent to the matter, concerning such things as the safety equipment on the *Sultana*, the condition of the boilers, whether it was overcrowded, or overloaded, and many other troubling facts.

Concerning the loading of the steamboat *Sultana* at Vicksburg, the Memphis *Daily Bulletin*, reported on May 21, 1865, that: "The safety of the boat was not particularly endangered by the number of men on board, but as there was no military necessity for placing them all upon one boat, the *Pauline Carroll*, being at the same time at Vicksburg with the *Sultana*, the men should have been divided."[17]

When the government finally closed the files on the riverboat *Sultana*, the army was exonerated of any wrong doing. The Washburn Commission, which had been formed to conduct the military inquiry, came to the conclusion that: "The evidence fully shows that the government has transferred as many or more troops on boats of no greater capacity than the *Sultana* frequently and with safety."[18]

It may be said that during wartime soldiers en route to the war effort were often packed aboard steamers, but in the case of the *Sultana*, the war was not an issue and its heavily loaded decks was not the cause of any military necessity. In the end, no amount of deliberation could bring back the poor souls who perished on the final voyage of the great side wheeler *Sultana*.

Almost 60 years after the saga of the Mississippi's *Titanic*, one of its survivors, James H. Kimberlin, spoke about the pangs he felt in his heart concerning the lack of attention over the *Sultana*: "The men who endured the torments of hell on earth, starved, famished from thirst, eaten with vermin, having endured all the indignities, insults and abuses possible for an armed bully to bestow upon them, to be so soon forgotten does not speak well for our government or the American people."[19]

Many factors may have contributed to the cause as to why the *Sultana* never became a household name. Even so, in Knoxville, Tennessee, at the Mount Olive Cemetery, on July

4, 1916, a *Sultana* monument was unveiled. In further remembrance, in 1989, another monument was erected at the Elmwood Cemetery in Memphis, Tennessee, "for those who died on the ill-fated passenger steamer *Sultana*." Yet again, the State of Mississippi at Vicksburg erected a *Sultana* State Historic Marker which was dedicated April 26-27-28, 2002; a 137 year anniversary in memory of the doomed passengers who died in the tragedy. As of yet, there is no National Monument for these Federal veterans of the Civil War.

Maybe in time, many will yet learn of the *Sultana* and how very much these forerunners gave of themselves in service to their country, so that the future of their descendants might hold the opportunity of a better life. Regardless of how the survivors felt about their circumstance, these brave men ran the course of life and finished the race with dignity.

Chapter 8

Life Goes On

As to all things, life goes on, even after an unforgettable tragedy. Such an event is very difficult for those who experienced it firsthand, but it is also hard on grieving friends and family members of the victims of tragedy. Time helps to heal wounds, but some scars can remain. Throughout the riverboat era, painful lessons were often learned, with the ever present dangers of fire, floating ice packs, snags, high winds and boiler explosions. Due to these perils, America's river highways of that time period, would teach its students the high cost of the convenience of luxurious steamboat travel; through visions of the dead and dying, the cries for help, the stench of burning flesh, and the drowning of hundreds who would meet eternity to frail to overcome the power of a mighty river flow.

The majority of passengers aboard the *Sultana* first survived as soldiers, where they witnessed the carnage of battle and innumerable hardships. Then, being taken prisoner, they endured death itself in all its frightful forms. Finally, with hope and sweet passions of life within the reach of possibility, suddenly, and without warning, the gates of hell were unleashed upon their patriotic souls. Scores horribly perished almost within sight of their own dreams and desires, but yet a few survived to continue their quest - the grail of humanity. A few are featured here in the following pages.

One man on the *Sultana* who, in at least one published account was numbered as having died on the steamer but was actually a survivor, went on to live a full life. His name was Reverend Emanuel Hush Yeisley.

Emanuel Yeisley was born in Amsterdam, Ohio, Licking County, November 12, 1840. His middle name of Hush was his mother's maiden name. In 1842, he moved with his parents to Ashland County, Ohio, then in 1845, Delaware County, and in 1851, to Van Wert County, where he stayed until the beginning of the Civil War. He enlisted in company G, 76th Regiment Ohio Volunteer Infantry on or about the 20th of November, 1861, in Jackson Town, Licking County, Ohio, where Yeisley would begin his amazing historical journey.[1]

Yeisley served his country during those long years of the Civil War, and he wrote about it in 1928 at his home in Ava, Missouri, saying in his own words: "About the last of January 1862 we started for the front we got to Fort Donalson in time for the battle just after fort henry had Surrendered and soon thru all the great Battles untill the Surrender of Atlanta Georgia then on the 27 of October on the range of loock out mountain I was taken prisoner..."[2]

He was imprisoned at the Cahaba Federal Prison, near Selma, Alabama, on the Alabama River, and was one of the many who endured Civil War prison life. Yeisley survived six months at Cahaba, and was paroled March 12, 1865. After his release he was taken to Vicksburg, Mississippi, where he boarded the doomed *Sultana.*[3]

After the boilers exploded Emanuel was thrown into the churning river and managed to get hold of two floating boards. The two boards were his lifeline, since he could not swim. He spent the night clinging to the boards, and at one point, had to fight for possession of one of them. Yeisley won the challenge, and the Mississippi claimed the other man. Emanuel was badly burned, on his chest and the lining of his nose, from the burst boiler and steam. He would carry the scars, physical and emotional, the remainder of his life.[4]

Later in 1865, Emanuel went on to marry Hettie Henney at Convoy, Ohio, having seven boys and four girls. It is not known if his almost miraculous salvation was a factor, but Emanuel Yeisley was converted to the Christian faith in 1866, and became a Minister of the Gospel with the Church of God. Later in life he devoted much of his time to the study of the works of various Bible students.[5]

The *Douglas County Herald*, published at Ava, Missouri, had this to say about the county's 25-year resident, Emanuel Yeisley: "Mr. Yeisley was the last commander of Andy Martin G.A.R. Post, the local organization of the Civil War Veterans. The post was disbanded at impressive services held in the high school building here in the fall of 1929. Mr. Yeisley presided at this meeting and delivered the address entrusting the records and files of the G.A.R. Post to the local Legion post. Sixteen Veterans of the Civil War were in attendance at his meeting...In his address before this last gathering of members of the G.A.R. Post, members of the American Legion, businessmen and citizens of Ava, Mr. Yeisley in a broken manner, due to his advanced age, reviewed many experiences of the Civil War and the early days of the Andy Martin Post to the delight of his audience."[6]

In his obituary, it read: "Civil War Veteran Dies August 27, 1931. E.H. Yeisley, 90 years old, buried Tuesday. Last commanding officer of the local G.A.R. - Presided when records were turned over to the legion. E.H. Yeisley, 90 years old, veteran of the Civil War, died at his home here early Monday morning. Short funeral services were conducted at his home Tuesday afternoon by Rev. John Silvey followed by burial in the Burdett Cemetery, four miles west of town [Ava, Missouri]. The American Legion had charge of the services at the grave and accorded the departed veteran a military funeral...Mr. Yeisley was born at Amsterdam, Ohio, November 12, 1840, being 90 years 9 months and 19 days of age. He enlisted in the Civil War at the beginning and served until its close. He was one of the few surviving the Sultana disaster on the Mississippi River at the close of the war. The Sultana, a river ship, was carrying Union soldiers northward on the Mississippi following the close of the war, when an explosion destroyed the ship and killed most of those on board..."

Another survivor of the *Sultana* was James Thomas Wolverton who (from U.S. records, TN & MS records, Tippah Co., MS records, McNairy Co., TN records, & family Bibles), was born December 31, 1844, in Tippah County, Mississippi, he died March 13, 1928.

James Thomas Wolverton grew up in Adamsville, Tennessee, where he went to school. At the age of 18, on September 15, 1862, he joined the Union army as a corporal in G Company, 6th Regiment, West Tennessee Cavalry Volunteers. (He was first drafted into the Confederate forces, but being opposed to slavery he ran away and volunteered to fight for the Union).

In a letter to the editor of the *Commercial Appeal*, Memphis, Tennessee, January 29, 1920, Wolverton writes: "Gentlemen: Having read in your paper of Jan. 25, 1920, a detailed history of the Sultana disaster, 9 miles above Memphis on April 27, 1865, it brought back to my mind that awful night of suffering and death.

"Capt. Woolridge has added some detailed accounts to the story I had not known. I was on board the ill-fated steamer at the time of the explosion. I was stationed on the hurricane deck on the east side (starboard) of the steamer near the center. Just behind me was a saloon and an ice chest. The water leaked from the chest and wet my blanket. I had no other place I could occupy, as every other place was crowded with human sleepers.

"As I said, every available space I could see was occupied by sleeping soldiers, perhaps dreaming of loved ones they would soon meet. Alas, what a terrible fate awaited them!

"While slumbering there, all at once I felt a terrible shock, followed by a deafening explosion...I went whirling down the river and soon landed in a drift with some others and went whirling in a circle. We could see the burning wreck of the steamer, then as the next view, the lights of Memphis, which looked like hundreds of stars beckoning to us.

"...Now, I cannot think of that terrible night of the disaster without deep sorrow. Oh, the terrible screams of the victims! They haunt me when I hear the incident mentioned. It was like an old camp meeting before the war when the preacher worked every soul up to shouting.

"I have two pictures of the Sultana, taken at Helena, showing her crowded condition. I boarded her at Vicksburg with many others. We had been confined at Cahawba Prison and exchanged at Vicksburg.

"The story of this disaster given by Capt. Woolridge is about correct. I never knew before what became of the hulk, and that the island disappeared. After remaining in the hospital for several days, I went to Camp Chase, Ohio, and from there to Pulaski, Tennessee, where my regiment was stationed and was discharged.

"I am now 77 years old and have lived at Adamsville, Tennessee, nearly all my life.

"The river was at its highest stage, thawing in the north. Two or three years ago the survivors held a meeting and reported that only about twelve of the survivors of the Sultana were living. But perhaps some other outside billy goats like myself did not know about the meeting. It is remarkable that any of us could be alive after such a great explosion and exposure to the ice-cold water." James T. Wolverton, Sergt., Co. G, 6th Tenn. Cav.

Horace May Wolverton, son of James Thomas Wloverton, wrote about his father's experiences on March 13, 1928, which read in part: "...James Thomas, my father, was a soldier in the Civil War...He became a member of the Sixth Tennessee Cavalry, under Captain Hurst. They rode after Forrest when he was at the height of his raids on the Union forces and their supplies. They fought the guerrillas which infested the country at that time.

"...Later, my father was captured in a skirmish with Confederate forces near Bolivar, Tenn. He was taken to Cohaba, Alabama, where he was imprisoned for several months in an old brick cotton warehouse made into a prison. Several hundred men were confined here. He was there when an effort was made by prisoners to tunnel out.

"...After seven months in this filthy prison he was sent in an exchange of Union and Confederate prisoners, headed for Camp Chase, Ohio. His group was transported over what is now the Southern Railway running to Memphis. They were then transferred to the steamboat Sultana...

"About nine or ten miles above Memphis, during the night, the boilers blew up and the boat sank, throwing everyone into the cold water...Father was greatly chilled but otherwise unhurt...A tender-hearted Rebel who was near at the time, took off his shirt and put it on my father. Dad tried his whole life to find out the name of this person, to no avail. He wanted to reward him for his kindness and to be his friend.

"...Father, in his later life, was very religious, going each day to his secret retreat in the woods to pray. I have been told by others they often ran onto him in the woods praying. He had purchased a flag a great many years before his death, to be placed on his coffin. He loved the flag so much that patriotism was almost a religion with him.

"The reason he assigned for fighting on the Northern side was the effort of the Confederacy to regulate the number of votes a person could cast to the benefit of the slave owner

--one vote for each slave owned. He often said he knew he'd be worse off than a slave under this system. He didn't believe in slavery.

"Father spelled his name with double-o, as Woolverton, until his discharge from the Union Army. His discharge papers spelled it with a single o, Wolverton, and ever afterward he spelled it that way. He must have enlisted as "Wolverton" to have been discharged as written. Many of the Wolvertons still carry the double-o." Horace May Wolverton, San Diego, California.

A letter written by another survivor, William Crisp, in his own words, on December 31st, 1910, from Osceola, Nebraska, also survives and is added here to his honor, it reads: "Comrade Yours in F. C. L. - William Crisp: Dear Comrade your letter received to night and was glad to get the letter from one that was on the ill-fated Sultana that night of darkness and Death in fire and water and men crushed beneath the Burning Timbers I never shall forget the word awful don't express it.

"I enlisted in the 18th Michigan Vol. Infantry at Hillsdale, Mich in August 1862 for three years during the war under Colonel Dolitle.

"We started on our campaign at Covington Kentucky and we drove the Rebels Back from there and we follered on to Atlanta and then we was sent back with General Tommas to Nashville Tenn that was 1864 while going back I was taken Prisoner the 24th of September 1864 and was sent to Cahawba Prison for seven months and was there until the war ended and then was taken to Vicksburg and then we loaded on the Sultana for St. Louis we had got to Memphis Tenn and Started from their about 12 o'clock and we got about nine or ten miles up the River when the Boiler exploded and the decks fell in and then the fire began to do its work.

"...You will remember when the water came into our prison don't you how men died in the water about five hundred men died then in that Hell Hole.

"After 12 days they took us out and then we started for Vicksburg. I never shall forget that awful night tongue cannot tell. It was the greatest marine disaster on record the greatest loss of life. I think nearly two thousand men perished that night out of all the men on the Sultana. There is about 27 of them living now near as we can tell. Oh, what a slaughter of human life after suffering what we did in that pen of Starvation and death you and me was in Cahawba Pen. We are out of the filthy place we are out of the ragging water to tell the horred story of degradation and death that we endured that this nation might live.

"All Hail to the Boys in Blue they have a name that will live as long as time does last. They was brave and true to there flag and there Country...

"I belong to Post No 36, Department of Nebraska am its Chaplin I remain your Comrade in F. C. L." William Crisp.

Afterwards, all of the *Sultana's* victims were left to carry on with its scars, which is evident in their passionate words, and they eventually formed an association where survivors gathered together to reminisce and be with others like themselves - to resurrect the memory of their fallen comrades who were less fortunate than they. In retrospect, the memories of such a terrible ordeal was very painful for survivors to conjure up. While the saga undoubtedly continued to play out in their minds for the rest of their lives, their desire would have surely been that others never cease to remember the poor lost souls of the *Sultana*; and that, God forbid, anything so unthinkable or unbearable could ever happen again.

A sermon given by Reverend Dr. George White at the Calvary Episcopal Church in Memphis, Tennessee, taken from the Memphis *Argus*, May 2, 1865, after the tragedy, reads in part:

"...the steamer was on her way, when suddenly the passengers are aroused to find themselves encompassed by fire. Who can tell the agony of that hour? What were the struggles of that hour; charred bodies, torn limbs, the agonizing cries; think of the loud shrieks ringing wildly over the Mississippi; cries for assistance from persons who had clung to such fragments of the wreck as they had grasped. Why attempt to describe such a scene, we are compelled to exclaim. Then arose that wild fearful shriek, then all was hushed save the wild wind and the remorseless dash of water, at intervals the solitary shrieks, the bubbling cry of some strong swimmer in his agonies..."

Author's
Final Word

After writing an article about the *Sultana's* extraordinary final voyage, and one of the survivors, Emanuel Hush Yeisley, for *The Ozarks Mountaineer* magazine, I was amazed to learn how few had ever heard of the event, even today. Many textbooks, libraries, and bookstores, seemed to have overlooked the compelling saga of the once grand riverboat steamer *Sultana,* and the many who perished; although there are several good books and articles that have been published.

My main objective in writing this book was to rekindle the flame of the forgotten heart rendering story that unraveled on the Mississippi River that April morning. I hoped by comparing other like tragedies, and reviewing the passengers' difficult journeys and experiences, the reader might more fully understand what sort of men these were (as a majority aboard)

65

who had perished. This was my focus.

Somewhere along the Mississippi in Arkansas, buried in the ground where the great river once flowed in 1865, is the grave of the *Sultana*. Some may have walked over it in recent years, not knowing what, or who, was entombed below them underground; or what terrible drama they were surrounded by - separated only by time.

So it is with the *Sultana*, buried in the quagmire of the past. Its pesky ghosts are still hauntingly real. The spooks and apparitions of an untimely death continue to rattle their chains, wanting only to be embraced by those who might have forgotten the *Titanic* of the Mississippi.

Acknowledgments

I would like to thank my wife Katherine, and sons Ryan, Seth and Eli, for all of their patience and support. Also, thanks to Barbara Wehrman, Dr. Fred Pfister, and everyone at *The Ozarks Mountaineer* magazine for all of their help. Thanks go to the generosity of Dorothy Schriever (great-granddaughter) and Joanne Todd Rabun (great-great-granddaughter) of Emanuel Yeisley. And, Jo Ann Hall, who provided materials about her distant relative, James Thomas Wolverton; and additional material concerning William Crisp. Thanks to the Neosho, Missouri, Newton County Library, and to everyone who gave their support.

A debt of gratitude is extended to all of the authors and publishers who provided the source materials used in this book. Without their pioneering efforts concerning the *Sultana*, and other related subjects, the work could not have been done. Special thoughts of thanksgiving are offered to the survivors who were brave enough to tell their stories and write them down.

I sincerely thank my father, to whom this book is dedicated, (along with the passengers of the *Sultana)*, for a lifetime of inspiration, with the hope that he would have approved of my recent endeavors.

Finally, thanks to Heritage Books Inc., who saw fit to further publish and document such history.

Author's sketch of the Lower Mississippi

Reverend Emanuel Hush Yeisley, Company G, 76th Ohio Volunteer
Infantry, survivor of the *Sultana* disaster. 1840-1931.
(Courtesy of Dorothy Shriever)

Emanuel H. Yeisley's tombstone at the Burdett Cemetery just west of Ava, Missouri. (Author's collection)

James Thomas Wolverton, Sergt., Co. G, 6th Tennessee Cavalry, survivor of the *Sultana*. (Courtesy of Jo Ann Hall)

Civil War soldiers became very familiar with the smoke and cannon-fire of fierce battle. (Re-enactment photo by the author)

Cavalryman and artilleryman played an important role in the Civil War, which accounted for many of the passengers aboard the ill-fated *Sultana*. (Re-enactment photo by the author)

The unfortunate dead littered many Civil War battlegrounds.
(Re-enactment photo by the author)

Chapter Notes

Chapter 1
Perilous Waters

1. *Titanic*, by Leo Marriott, Smithmark Publishers 1997

2. Funk & Wagnells New Encyclopedia, Funk & Wagnells, Inc. 1979; Marriott

3. Ibid.

4. *Sinking of the Titanic*, by Jay Henry Mowbray, Geo. W. Bertron 1912

5. Ibid.

6. Ibid.

7. Ibid.

8. Ibid.

9. *Lost Liners*, by Peter Schnall, Rob Kuhns, Patrick Prentice, Robert D. Ballard and Barbara Earle Ballard, Partisan Pictures, Inc. 2000

10. Funk & Wagnells

11. *Saluda* Memorial, Lexington, Missouri

12. *Lexington Journal*, April 14, 1852

13. *Life on the Mississippi*, by Mark Twain, Hartford: American Publishing Company 1883

14. *Missouri Republican*, June 16, 1858

Chapter 2
Long Hard Journey

1. *The First Step in the War*, by Stephen D. Lee, Battles and Leaders of the Civil War, Vol. 1, The Century Company 1887

2. *The History of the Unites States*, by William Backus Guitteau, Houghton Mifflin Company 1942

3. Ibid.

4. Ibid.

5. *The Confederate Retreat from Gettysburg*, by John D. Imboden, Battles and Leaders of the Civil War, Vol. 3, The Century Company 1887

6. *Notes of Cold Harbor*, by George Cary Eggleston, Battles and Leaders of the Civil War, Vol. 4, The Century Company 1887

7. *From the Wilderness to Cold Harbor*, by E.M. Law, Battles and Leaders of the Civil War, Vol. 4, The Century Company 1887

8. *Pen and Powder*, by Franc B. Wilkie, Ticknor and Company, Boston 1888

9. *The Mississippi Valley in the Civil War*, by John Fiske, Houghton, Mifflin and Company, Boston and New York 1900

10. *Recollections of the Civil War*, by Charles A. Dana, D. Appleton and Company, New York 1889

11. *Disaster, Struggle, Triumph: The Adventures of 1000 "Boys In Blue,"* by Mrs. Arabella M. Willson, C.A. Richardson, Albany: The Argus Company, Printers 1870

12. *With the Cavalry on the Peninsula,* by William W. Averell, Battles and Leaders of the Civil War, Vol. 2, The Century Company 1887

13. *Antietam Scenes,* by Charles Carleton Coffin, Battles and Leaders of the Civil War, The Century Company 1887

14. *The Battle of Malvern Hill,* by Fitz John Porter, Battles and Leaders of the Civil War, The Century Company 1887

Chapter 3
Hellholes of War

1. Andersonville Civil War Prison, Southwest Archaeological Center

2. *The Sultana Tragedy,* by Jerry O. Potter, Pelican Publishing Company, 1992

3. *A Prisoner of War in Virginia 1864-5,* by George Haven-Putnam, G.P. Putnam's Sons, New York and London, The Knickerbocker Press 1914

4. Ibid.

5. Ibid.

6. *The Soldier's Story,* by Warren Lee Goss, Boston: Lee and Shepard 1869

7. Ibid.

8. Ibid.

9. Ibid.

10. Ibid.

11. *Battle Cry of Freedom: The Civil War Era,* by James M. McPherson, Oxford University Press 1988

12. *Cahaba - A Story of Captive Boys in Blue,* by Jesse Hawes, Burr Printing House, New York 1888; *Cahaba Prison and the Sultana Disaster,* by John L. Walker, Hamilton, Ohio, Brown & Whitaker 1910

13. R.M. Whitfield, Cahaba's Chief Surgeon, March 13, 1864; OR, Ser. 2, 6:1124-25

14. *James Thomas Wolverton,* by Horace May Wolverton, March 13, 1928; Courtesy Jo Ann Hall

Chapter 4
Headlines

1. *The Surrender at Appomattox Court House,* by Horace Porter, Battles and Leaders of the Civil War, Vol. 4, The Century Company 1887

2. Funk & Wagnells, Funk & Wagnells, Inc., New York 1979; *Abraham Lincoln: His Story in His Own Words,* by Ralph Geoffrey Newman, Doubleday & Company, Inc., Garden City, New York 1975; *The Day Lincoln Was Shot,* by Jim Bishop, Harper & Row Publishers, New York and Evanston 1955

3. Ibid.

4. *Recollections of the Civil War,* by Charles A. Dana, D. Appleton and Company, New York 1898

5. Ibid.

Chapter 5
Advent of the Sultana

1. Funk & Wagnells, Funk & Wagnells, Inc., New York 1979; Microsoft Encarta Encyclopedia, Microsoft Corporation 2000

2. Ibid.

3. Ibid.

4. Cincinnati *Daily Commercial*, February 4, 1863

5. Ibid; *Cahaba Prison and the Sultana Disaster,* by William O. Bryant, University of Alabama Press, Tuscaloosa & London 1990

6. Cincinnati *Daily Commercial,* February 4, 1863; *Transport to Disaster,* by James W. Elliott, Holt, Rinehart and Winston, Inc., New York, New York 1962

7. Elliott

8. Ibid.

9. Ibid.

10. Ibid.

11. *Death on the Dark River,* by Cedric A. Larson, American Heritage, October 1955

12. Report to Secretary of War Stanton by "Brevet Brigadier General W. Hoffman Commissary General of Prisoners," May 7, 1865; *The Sultana Tragedy,* by Jerry O. Potter, Pelican Publishing Company, Gretna 1992; Elliott

13. Report of Major General Dana "Headquarters Department of Mississippi," Vicksburg, May 8, 1865, to Brigadier-General W. Hoffman, Commissary-General of Prisoners; *Loss of the Sultana and Reminiscences of Survivors,* by Chester D. Berry, Darius D. Thorp, Lansing, Michigan 1892

14. Ibid.

15. *Yorktown and Williamsburg,* by Warren Lee Goss, Battles and Leaders of the Civil War, Vol. 2, The Century Company 1887

16. Berry

17. The *Plainsville Times,* by James R. Collins, Plainsville, Kansas, May 28, 1908

18. Berry

19. Ibid.

20. Berry; Elliott; Potter

21. Ibid.

22. Ibid.

23. Ibid.

Chapter 6
Voices of the Past

1. *Sultana Saga: The Eventful Life and Times of Reverend Emanuel Hush Yeisley,* by Rex Jackson, The Ozarks Mountaineer magazine, April/May 2001

2. Ibid.

3. *Loss of the Sultana and Reminiscences of Survivors*, by Chester D. Berry, Lansing, Michigan 1892

4. Ibid.

5. Ibid.

6. *Cahaba - A Story of Captive Boys in Blue*, by Jesse Hawes, New York 1888

7. Berry

8. James Thomas Wolverton, *Commercial Appeal*, Memphis, Tennessee, January 29, 1920, Courtesy Jo Ann Hall

9. Letter written by William Crisp, December 31, 1910, Osceola, Nebraska, Courtesy Jo Ann Hall

10. Berry

11. Hawes

12. *Transport to Disaster*, by James W. Elliott, Holt, Rinehart and Winston 1962

13. *The Sultana Disaster*, by Joseph Taylor Elliott, Indiana Historical Society Publications, Vol. V, No. 3, 1913

14. *The Destruction of the Sultana*, by J.H. Kimberlin, Hamilton 1910

15. *Cahaba Prison and the Sultana Disaster*, by William O. Bryant, The University of Alabama Press, Tuscaloosa and London 1990

16. Memphis *Commercial Appeal*, January 25, 1920

17. Berry

18. Elliott

Chapter 7
Pangs of Recovery

1. *Military Hospitals in Memphis, 1861-1865*, LaPointe

2. *Loss of the Sultana and Reminiscences of Survivors*, by Chester D. Berry, Lansing, Michigan 1892

3. Memphis *Argus*, May 12, 1865

4. *Transport to Disaster*, by James W. Elliott, Holt, Rinehart and Winston, Inc., New York, N.Y. 1962

5. *National Tribune*, April 18, 1889

6. Berry

7. Ibid.

8. Way, *Directory of Western River Packets*; Elliott

9. *Fifty Years on the Mississippi: Gould's History of River Navigation*, by Emerson W. Gould, St. Louis, Nixon Jones Printing Company 1889

10. *The Sultana Tragedy*, by Jerry O. Potter, Pelican Publishing Company, Gretna 1992

11. Memphis *Daily Bulletin*, May 27, 1865

12. *The Titanic: The Extraordinary Story of the "Unsinkable" Ship*, by Geoff Tibballs, The Readers Digest Association, Inc., Pleasantville, New York/Montreal 1997

13. Ibid.

14. Ibid.

15. Ibid.

16. Potter

17. Memphis *Daily Bulletin*, May 21, 1865

18. Ibid.

19. *The Destruction of the Sultana*, by J.H. Kimberlin, Hamilton 1910

Chapter 8
Life Goes On

1. *Sultana Saga: The Eventful Life And Times of Reverend Emanuel Hush Yeisley*, by Rex Jackson, The Ozark Mountaineer magazine, April/May 2001

2. Ibid.

3. Ibid.

4. Ibid.

5. Ibid.

6. Ibid.

Note: Information pertaining to Emanuel Hush Yeisley was furnished courtesy of Dorothy Schriever (great granddaughter) and Joanne Todd Rabun (great great granddaughter) of Mr. Yeisley. Also, material concerning James Thomas Wolverton and the letter to him from William Crisp was contributed by Jo Ann Hall, distant relative of Mr. Wolverton.

Bibliography

Averell, William W., *With the Cavalry on the Peninsula,* Battles and Leaders of the Civil War, Vol. 2, The Century Company 1887

Berry, Chester D., *Loss of the Sultana and Reminiscences of Survivors,* Lansing, Michigan 1892

Bishop, Jim, *The Day Lincoln Was Shot,* Harper and Row Publishers, New York and Evanston 1955

Bryant, William O., *Cahaba Prison and the Sultana Disaster,* University of Alabama Press 1990

Coffin, Charles C., *Antietam Scenes,* Battles and Leaders of the Civil War, The Century Company 1887

Dana, Charles A., *Recollections of the Civil War,* D. Appleton and Company, New York 1889

Eggleston, George C., *Notes of Cold Harbor,* Battles and Leaders of the Civil War, Vol. 4, The Century Company 1887

Elliott, James W., *Transport to Disaster,* Holt, Rinehart and Winston, Inc., New York, N.Y. 1962

Fiske, John, *The Mississippi Valley in the Civil War,* Houghton, Mifflin and Company, Boston and New York 1900

Goss, Warren L., *The Soldier's Story,* Boston: Lee and Shepard 1869; *Yorktown and Williamsburg,* Battles and Leaders of the Civil War, Vol. 2, The Century Company 1887

Gould, Emerson W., *Fifty Years on the Mississippi: Gould's History of River Navigation,* St. Louis, Nixon Jones Printing

Company 1889

Guitteau, William B., *The History of the United States*, Houghton Mifflin Company 1942

Hawes, Jesse, *Cahaba - A Story of Captive Boys in Blue*, New York 1888

Imboden, John D., *The Confederate Retreat From Gettysburg*, Battles and Leaders of the Civil War, Vol. 3, The Century Company 1887

Jackson, Rex T., *Sultana Saga: The Eventful Life of Reverend Emanuel Hush Yeisley*, The Ozarks Mountaineer magazine, April/May 2001

Kimberlin, J.H., *The Destruction of the Sultana*, Hamilton 1910

Larson, Cedric A., *Death on the Dark River*, American Heritage, October 1955

Law, E.M., *From the Wilderness to Cold Harbor*, Battles and Leaders of the Civil War, Vol. 4, The Century Company 1887

Lee, Stephen D., *The First Step in the War*, Battles and Leaders of the Civil War, Vol. 1, The Century Company 1887

Marriott, Leo, *Titanic*, Smithmark Publishers 1997

McPherson, James M., *Battle Cry of Freedom - The Civil War Era*, Oxford University Press 1988

Mowbray, Jay H., *Sinking of the Titanic*, Geo. W. Berton 1912

Newman, Ralph G., *Abraham Lincoln - His Story in His Own Words*, Doubleday & Company, Inc., Garden City, New York 1975

Porter, Fitz J., *Battle of Malvern Hill*, Battles and Leaders of the Civil War, The Century Company 1887

Porter, Horace, *The Surrender at Appomattox Court House*, Battles and Leaders of the Civil War, The Century Company 1887

Potter, Jerry O., *The Sultana Tragedy*, Pelican Publishing Company, Gretna 1992

Putnam, George H., *A Prisoner of War in Virginia 1864-5*, G.P. Putnam's Sons, New York and London, The Knickerbocker Press 1914

Tibballs, Geoff, *The Titanic: The Extraordinary Story of the "Unsinkable" Ship*, Reader's Digest Association, Inc. 1997

Twain, Mark, *Life on the Mississippi*, American Publishing Company, Hartford 1883

Wilkie, Franc B., *Pen and Powder*, Ticknor and Company, Boston 1888

Willson, Arabella M., *Disaster, Struggle, Triumph: The Adventures of a 1000 "Boys In Blue,"* C.A. Richardson, Albany: The Argus Company, Printers 1870

Newspapers and Other Sources

1. Andersonville Civil War Prison - Southeast Archaeological Center
2. Cincinnati *Daily Commercial*, February 4, 1863
3. Collins, James R., The *Plainsville Times*, Plainsville, Kansas, May 28, 1908
4. *Commercial Appeal*, Memphis, Tennessee, January 25 and 29, 1920
5. Crisp, William, Osceola, Nebraska, a letter dated December 31, 1910; Courtesy of Jo Ann Hall
6. *Douglas County Herald*, Ava, Missouri, 1929
7. Funk & Wagnells New Encyclopedia, Funk & Wagnells, Inc, 1979
8. General W. Hoffman Commissary General of Prisoners, May 7, 1865
9. *Lexington Journal* as quoted in the *St. Joseph Gazette*, April 14, 1852
10. *Lost Liners*, Robert D. Ballard, Barbara Earle Ballard, Peter Schnall, Rob Kuhns and Patrick Prentice, Partisan Pictures, Inc. 2000
11. Major General Dana "Headquarters Department of Mississippi," Vicksburg, May 8, 1865
12. Memphis *Argus*, May 12, 1865
13. Memphis *Daily Bulletin*, May 21 and 27, 1865
14. Microsoft Encarta Encyclopedia, Microsoft Corporation, 2000
15. *Missouri Republican*, statement of Mr. W.G. Mepham, June 16, 1858
16. *National Tribune*, April 18, 1889

17. Steamboat *Saluda* Memorial, Lexington, Missouri

18. Whitfield, R.M., Cahaba's Chief Surgeon, March 1864

19. Wolverton, Horace May, *Commercial Appeal*, Memphis, Tennessee, January 29, 1920; Courtesy Jo Ann Hall

20. Yeisley, Emanuel Hush; Courtesy Dorothy Schriever, Joanne Todd Rabun

Chronology

1786 - Earliest recorded steam powered riverboat
August 17, 1807 - 1st steam powered commercial riverboat
May 24, 1819 - 1st steam powered transatlantic ship
April 12, 1861 - Fort Sumter
April 14, 1861 - Fall of Fort Sumter and beginning of the Civil War
July 16, 1861 - 1st Battle of Manassas (Bull Run)
January 3, 1863 - Launching of the *Sultana*
Mid-1863 - Cahaba prison opens around June
January 1864 - Andersonville prison begins
April 9, 1865 - End of the Civil War
April 14, 1865 - President Abraham Lincoln is shot
April 15, 1865 - Abraham Lincoln dies at 7:20 a.m.
April 15, 1865 - *Sultana* leaves Cairo, Illinois, heading south
April 19, 1865 - *Sultana* reaches New Orleans, Louisiana
April 21, 1865 - *Sultana* leaves New Orleans headed north
April 23, 1865 - *Sultana* arrives in Vicksburg, Mississippi;
                         boiler is repaired; takes on parolee's
April 26, 1865 - Docks in Helena, Arkansas, in the morning;

Sultana photo is taken
April 26, 1865 - John Wilkes Booth is killed
April 26, 1865 - *Sultana* docks in Memphis, Tennessee, at 6:30 p.m.
April 26, 1865 - *Sultana,* around midnight, takes on coal (west bank)
April 27, 1865 - 1:00 a.m., the *Sultana* heads north
April 27, 1865 - 2:00 a.m., the *Sultana's* boilers explode

OFFICIAL LIST OF EXCHANGED PRISONERS ON THE BOAT

McCutcheon, W., Private, Company C, 2nd Indiana Cavalry
Phillips, Wm., Private, Company C, 2nd Indiana Cavalry
Young, J., Private, Company C, 2nd Indiana Cavalry
Hardin, L.D., Private, Company D, 2nd Indiana Cavalry
Lidd, L.D., Private, Company D, 2nd Indiana Cavalry
Stevens, W., Private, Company D, 2nd Indiana Cavalry
Brown, J., Private, Company G, 2nd Indiana Cavalry
Bummerville, P.S., Private, Company K, 2nd Indiana Cavalry
Dillander, J., Private, Company C, 3rd Indiana Cavalry
Keorney, M., Private, Company C, 3rd Indiana Cavalry
Congers, Wm., Private, Company D, 3rd Indiana Cavalry
Noorier, J., Private, Company F, 3rd Indiana Cavalry
Raina, Wm., Private, Company C, 4th Indiana Cavalry
Simpkins, O.E., Private, Company C, 4th Indiana Cavalry
Franklin, B., Sergeant, Company F, 4th Indiana Cavalry
Trumball, A., Sergeant, Company F, 4th Indiana Cavalry
Evermore, N.D., Private, Company F, 4th Indiana Cavalry
Grubbs, Iaaac, Private, Company A, 5th Indiana Cavalry
Williams, N.S., Private, Company B, 5th Indiana Cavalry
Dean, J.D., Sergeant, Company C, 6th Indiana Cavalry
Milott, R.A., Corporal, Company D, 5th Indiana Cavalry
Thevin, A., Corporal, Company E, 5th Indiana Cavalry
McCullough, S.A., Private, Company H, 5th Indiana Cavalry
Evans, D.W., Private, Company L, 5th Indiana Cavalry
McBride, G., Private, Company L, 5th Indiana Cavalry
Mullen, J., Private, Company L, 5th Indiana Cavalry
Richardson, A., Private, Company L, 5th Indiana Cavalry
Scott, L., Private, Company L, 5th Indiana Cavalry
Applegate, J.B., Private, Company C, 6th Indiana Cavalry

Poterlield, W., Private, Company C, 6th Indiana Cavalry
O'Brien, P., Private, Company D, 6th Indiana Cavalry
Scole, R., Private, Company D, 6th Indiana Cavalry
Lee, E.C., Private, Company E, 6th Indiana eavain
Hobi, A.P., Sergeant, Company F, 6th Indiana Cavalry
Shal, F., Private, Company G, 6th Indiana Cavalry
Davis, J.W., Private, Company I, 6th Indiana Cavalry
Clearly, C.D., Sergeant, Company K, 6th Indiana Cavalry
Gathman, J.H., Private, Company L, 8th Indiana Cavalry
Hall, J.F., Private, Company C, 7th ndiana Cavalry
Nemier, Jas., Private, Company C, 7th Indiana Cavalry
Rowe, D.B., Private, Company C, 7th Indiana Cavalry
Sholey, P., Private, Company C, 7th Indiana Cavalry
Farrell, Jno., Private, Company D, 7th Indiana Cavalry
Frederick, G., Private, Company D, 7th Indiana Cavalry
Ames, S.P., Private, Company E, 7th Indiana Cavalry
Brocklon, J., Private, Company E, 7th Indiana Cavalry
Dany, B., Private, Company E, 7th Indiana Cavalry
Hachsell, J.L., Private, Company E, 7th Indiana Cavalry
Porter, C., Private, Company E, 7th Indiana Cavalry
Corlin, W.S., Private, Company E, 7th Indiana Cavalry
Nichols, C., Private, Company G, 7th Indiana Cavalry
Armstrong, B.B., Private, Company I, 7th Indiana Cavalry
Barrack, W., Private, Company I, 7th Indiana Cavalry
Swords, E., Private, Company I, 7th Indiana Cavalry
Elkin, F.M., Private, Company I, 7th Indiana Cavalry
Gard, W., Private, Company K, 7th Indiana Cavalry
Scott, Wm W., Private, Company K, 7th Indiana Cavalry
Smith, J., Private, Company K, 7th Indiana Cavalry
Johnson, H., Private, Company K, 7th Indiana Cavalry
McKann, A., Private, Company M, 7th Indiana Cavalry
Thompson, Wm E., Private, Company M, 7th Indiana Cavalry
Berry, W., Private, Company M, 7th Indiana Cavalry
Markabee, W., Private, Company B, 8th Indiana Cavalry
Millhen, E., Private, Company C, 8th Indiana Cavalry

Stiles, J.W., Private, Company F, 8th Indiana Cavalry
Fry, A., Private, Company F, 8th Indiana Cavalry
Talbrook, R., Private, Company H, 8th Indiana Cavalry
Madduy, Private, Company H, 8th Indiana Cavalry
Demis, Thos., Private, Company I, 8th Indiana Cavalry
Smith, C., Private, Company M, 8th Indiana Cavalry
Curtis, Daniel, Sergeant, Company A, 9th Indiana Cavalry
Spades, Jacob, Sergeant, Company A, 9th Indiana Cavalry
Day, E.R., Corporal, Company A, 9th Indiana Cavalry
Day, Pat, Private, Company A, 9th Indiana Cavalry
Evans, Chas., Private, Company A, 9th Indiana Cavalry
Paul, A.H., Private, Company A, 9th Indiana Cavalry
Riley, Wm., Private, Company A, 9th Indiana Cavalry
Talkington, Robt., Private, Company A, 9th Indiana Cavalry
Blessing, F., Corporal, Company B, 9th Indiana Cavalry
Mooney, Jno., Private, Company B, 9th Indiana Cavalry
Parmer, E.B., Private, Company B, 9th Indiana Cavalry
Reed, W.P., Private, Company B, 9th Indiana Cavalry
Sears, C.H., Private, Company B, 9th Indiana Cavalry
Scott, Robt., Private, Company B, 9th Indiana Cavalry
Stewart, Jno., Private, Company B, 9th Indiana Cavalry
Waller, P.J., Private, Company B, 9th Indiana Cavalry
Warner, W.C., Private, Company B, 9th Indiana Cavalry
Hawkins, A.W., Corporal, Company C, 9th Indiana Cavalry
Krammer, Thos., Private, Company C, 9th Indiana Cavalry
Collins, W.J., Corporal, Company D, 9th Indiana Cavalry
Church, C.C., Private, Company E, 9th Indiana Cavalry
Gilberth, Robt., Private, Company E, 9th Indiana Cavalry
Lasboytox, Private, Company E, 9th Indiana Cavalry
McCormack, A., Private, Company E, 9th Indiana Cavalry
Wood, E., Private, Company E, 9th Indiana Cavalry
Penson, Anderson, Private, Company F, 9th Indiana Cavalry
Graves, W.H., Sergeant, Company G, 9th Indiana Cavalry
Rodfinch, N.Z., Sergeant, Company G, 9th Indiana Cavalry
Abbison, H., Corporal, Company G, 9th Indiana Cavalry

Nation, E.K., Corporal, Company G, 9th Indiana Cavalry
Peacock, W.H., Private, Company G, 9th Indiana Cavalry
Allom, J.C., Private, Company G, 9th Indiana Cavalry
Clivinger, C.W., Private, Company G, 9th Indiana Cavalry
Downing, Geo., Private, Company G, 9th Indiana Cavalry
Hoober, M.C., Private, Company G, 9th Indiana Cavalry
Hooman, W.H., Private, Company G, 9th Indiana Cavalry
Johnson, L., Private, Company G, 9th Indiana Cavalry
King, C., Private, Company G, 9th Indiana Cavalry
Maynard, J.M., Private, Company G, 9th Indiana Cavalry
Reasoner, J.R., Private, Company G, 9th Indiana Cavalry
Swain, E.H., Lieutenant, Company G, 9th Indiana Cavalry
Thornbury, N., Lieutenant, Company G, 9th Indiana Cavalry
Marity, W.J., Sergeant, Company H, 9th Indiana Cavalry
Ballenger, F., Private, Company H, 9th Indiana Cavalry
Bell, Jas., Private, Company H, 9th Indiana Cavalry
Blake, Geo., Private, Company H, 9th Indiana Cavalry
Block, Wm., Private, Company H, 9th Indiana Cavalry
Brown, Wm., Private, Company H, 9th Indiana Cavalry
Chana, W.H., Private, Company H, 9th Indiana Cavalry
Delano, G.W., Private, Company H, 9th Indiana Cavalry
Dunham, A., Private, Company H, 9th Indiana Cavalry
McGinnis, S.S., Private, Company H, 9th Indiana Cavalry
Harden, W.H., Private, Company H, 9th Indiana Cavalry
Pratt, J., Private, Company H, 9th Indiana Cavalry
Shul, Jno., Private, Company H, 9th Indiana Cavalry
Stoops, H., Private, Company H, 9th Indiana Cavalry
Hawthorn, D.F., Sergeant, Company I, 9th Indiana Cavalry
Foldermar, B., Corporal, Company K, 9th Indiana Cavalry
Bailey, H., Private, Company K, 9th Indiana Cavalry
Emmons, J.W., Private, Company K, 9th Indiana Cavalry
Fisher, G.S., Private, Company K, 9th Indiana Cavalry
Gaston, S.M., Private, Company K, 9th Indiana Cavalry
Green, Seth J., Private, Company K, 9th Indiana Cavalry
Heard, J., Private, Company K, 9th Indiana Cavalry

Laughton, T.P., Private, Company K, 9th Indiana Cavalry
Lewis, Jno. B., Private, Company K, 9th Indiana Cavalry
Masler, P., Private, Company K, 9th Indiana Cavalry
Newton, H.O., Private, Company K, 9th Indiana Cavalry
Rea, W.T., Private, Company K, 9th Indiana Cavalry
Sawant, J., Private, Company K, 9th Indiana Cavalry
Shenler, T.D., Company K, 9th Indiana Cavalry
Shockly, G.H., Private, Company K, 9th Indiana Cavalry
Stevens, D., Private, Company K, 9th Indiana Cavalry
Stocker, Jas., Private, Company K, 9th Indiana Cavalry
Winterhost, J., Private, Company K, 9th Indiana Cavalry
Zix, M., Private, Company K, 9th Indiana Cavalry
Boner, Jno., Sergeant, Company L, 9th Indiana Cavalry
Woorhouse, R.A., Sergeant, Company L, 9th Indiana Cavalry
Grevell, N.E., Corporal, Company L, 9th Indiana Cavalry
Alexander, J.D., Private, Company L, 9th Indiana Cavalry
McCartney, L., Private, Company L, 9th Indiana Cavalry
Christian, J.J., Private, Company L, 9th Indiana Cavalry
Doggy, G. W., Private, Company L, 9th Indiana Cavalry
Isentredge, J.M., Private, Company L, 9th Indiana Cavalry
Johnston, J.F., Private, Company L, 9th Indiana Cavalry
Johnston, W.F., Private, Company L, 9th Indiana Cavalry
Kelly, S., Private, Company L, 9th Indiana Cavalry
Miller, Elias, Private, Company L, 9th Indiana Cavalry
Molway, C., Private, Company L, 9th Indiana Cavalry
Ring, S., Private, Company L, 9th Indiana Cavalry
Smith, L., Private, Company L, 9th Indiana Cavalry
Spacy, O.F., Private, Company L, 9th Indiana Cavalry
Windser, W.H., Private, Company L, 9th Indiana Cavalry
Gaskill, David, Sergeant, Company M, 9th Indiana Cavalry
Armstrong, J., Corporal, Company M, 9th Indiana Cavalry
Bragg, W., Corporal, Company M, 9th Indiana Cavalry
Hoffman, W.H., Private, Company M, 9th Indiana Cavalry
Ridley, F., Private, Company M, 9th Indiana Cavalry
Watson, J., Private, Company M, 9th Indiana Cavalry

Baker, O., Private, Company M, 9th Indiana Cavalry
Jolly, B.B., Sgt. Major, Company K, 10th Indiana Cavalry
Crawford, E.T., Hos Steward, Co. H, 10th Indiana Cavalry
Dixon, W.F., Lieutenant, Company A, 10th Indiana Cavalry
Bedman, J., Corporal, Company A, 10th Indiana Cavalry
Barlow, J., Private, Company A, 10th Indiana Cavalry
Reives, Thos., Lieutenant, Company C, 10th Indiana Cavalry
Smith, W.B., Corporal, Company C, 10th Indiana Cavalry
Farrell, M., Sergeant, Company D, 10th Indiana Cavalry
Graham, J., Private, Company G, 10th Indiana Cavalry
McKenzie, J., Private, Company G, 10th Indiana Cavalry
McLelland, J., Private, Company G, 10th Indiana Cavalry
Kelly, G.W., Private, Company H, 10th Indiana Cavalry
Sanford, G.W., Private, Company H, 10th Indiana Cavalry
Bindle, R., Private, Company H, 10th Indiana Cavalry
Twigg, A.G., Lieutenant, Company K, 10th Indiana Cavalry
Mills, C.W., Sergeant, Company K, 10th Indiana Cavalry
Jones, J.T., Private, Company K, 10th Indiana Cavalry
Gaffney, M., Captain, Company L, 10th Indiana Cavalry
Crawler, Jacob, Private, Company L, 10th Indiana Cavalry
Long, Henry M., Private, Company E, 11th Indiana Cavalry
Morgan, F., Private, Company F, 11th Indiana Cavalry
Keeler, L.L., Sergeant, Company H, 11th Indiana Cavalry
Clansville, G., Private, Company F, 12th Indiana Cavalry
Kline, Henry, Private, Company G, 12th Indiana Cavalry
Mitchell, J., Private, Company A, 13th Indiana Cavalry
Sutton, W., Private, Company A, 13th Indiana Cavalry
Baker, M.T., Private, Company B, 13th Indiana Cavalry
Brother, H., Private, Company G, 13th Indiana Cavalry
Holmes, W., Private, Company G, 13th Indiana Cavalry
Owens, M.J., Sergeant, Company I, 13th Indiana Cavalry
Whitesoll, J., Private, Company K, 13th Indiana Cavalry
Johnson, T.B., Private, Company D, 13th Indiana Cavalry
Lahue, C.J., Private, Company D, 13th Indiana Cavalry
Wadford, W., Private, Company M, 13th Indiana Cavalry

Lewis, Wm., Private, Company E, 16th Indiana Cavalry
Thahbonger, J.W., Private, Company A, 17th Indiana Cavalry
Stockman, B., Private, Company G, 17th Indiana Cavalry
Evens, G., Private, Company G, 17th Indiana Cavalry
Sampson, B.H., Corporal, Company I, 17th Indiana Cavalry
Fantinger, J.H., Private, Company I, 17th Indiana Cavalry
Caup, M.V., Private, Company H, 20th Indiana
Ashley, Y.K., 20th Indiana
Patrick, M., Private, Company H, 22nd Indiana Infantry
Smith, E.J., Private, Company D, 23rd Indiana Infantry
Conner, Wm., Private, 24th Indiana
Vesser, Sam, Private, Company K, 26th Indiana Infantry
Hershe, W.B., Private, Company A 29th Indiana
Brown, J., Sergeant, Company C, 29th Indiana
Aldfant, S.M., Private, Company D, 30th Indiana Infantry
Morris, S., Private, Company D, 30th Indiana Infantry
Dawson, G.W., Private, Company G, 30th Indiana Infantry
Beard, O.S., Private, Company I, 31st Indiana Infantry
Huber, E., Private, Company A, 32nd Indiana Infantry
Shoemaker, P., Private, Company B, 32nd Indiana Infantry
Shemire, L., Private, Company K, 32nd Indiana Infantry
Rass, C.P., Private, Company A, 34th Indiana Infantry
Tanam, M.O., Sergeant, Company B, 35th Indiana Infantry
Linch, Thos., Private, Company B, 35th Indiana Infantry
Donald, E.O., Private, Company D, 35th Indiana Infantry
Mulvany, P., Private, Company D, 35th Indiana Infantry
Crum, A.H., Private, Company G, 35th Indiana Infantry
McQuire, M., Private, Company G, 35th Indiana Infantry
Martin, J., Corporal, Company K, 35th Indiana Infantry
Beal, W., Private, Company B, 36th Indiana Infantry
Janey, J.R., Private, Company B, 36th Indiana Infantry
Pike, L., Sergeant, Company G, 37th Indiana Infantry
Taylor, S.A., Corporal, Company G, 37th Indiana Infantry
Cleveland, N., Private, Company A, 38th Indiana Infantry
Kelum, Martin, Private, Company D, 38th Indiana Infantry

Nash, Thos., Private, Company H, 38th Indiana Infantry
Slatting, J.W.H., Private, Company H, 38th Indiana Infantry
Monsort, R., Corporal, Company A, 40th Indiana Infantry
Thorn, T.J., Private, Company A, 40th Indiana Infantry
Howard, Jno., Private, Company C, 40th Indiana Infantry
Westh, Jno., Private, Company C, 40th Indiana Infantry
Kent, G.A., Sergeant, Company D, 40th Indiana Infantry
Nisley, C.M., Sergeant, Company D, 40th Indiana Infantry
Coleman, W.L., Private, Company D, 40th Indiana Infantry
Guear, Stephen, Private, Company F, 40th Indiana Infantry
Hiner, S.C., Corporal, Company G, 40th Indiana Infantry
Carr, J.M., Private, Company G, 40th Indiana Infantry
May, Chas., Private, Company G, 40th Indiana Infantry
Thompson, Jno., Private, Company G, 40th Indiana Infantry
Cook, W.A., Private, Company H, 40th Indiana Infantry
Jackson, Jas. H., Private, Company H, 40th Indiana Infantry
Meyer, J., Private, Company H, 40th Indiana Infantry
Ellenberger, J.M., Private, Company I, Indiana Infantry
Sloan, D.W., Private, Company I, Indiana Infantry
Hall, H., Private, Company K, 40th Indiana Infantry
Haspilk, H.L., Private, Company K, 40th Indiana Infantry
Smith, J., Corporal, Company A, 42nd Indiana Infantry
McFarland, W., Private, Company A, 42nd Indiana Infantry
Crabs, J., Private, Company C, 47th Indiana Infantry
Goers, W., Private, Company C, 47th Indiana Infantry
Marim, Wm., Private, Company C, 47th Indiana Infantry
Stendevant, T., Private, Company D, 53rd Indiana Infantry
Versey, J., Private, Company D, 53rd Indiana Infantry
Fletcher, J.M., Corporal, Company A, 57th Indiana Infantry
Yekk, J.A., Private, Company B, 57th Indiana Infantry
Bealer, G.W., Private, Company C, 57th Indiana Infantry
Lamb, M., Private, Company C, 57th Indiana Infantry
May, J.T., Private Company C, 57th Indiana Infantry
Newbern, E., Private, Company C, 57th Indiana Infantry
Smith, A., Private, Company C, 57th Indiana Infantry

Kibbee, J.H., Private Company D, 57th Indiana Infantry
Van Magg, I., Private, Company D, 57th Indiana Infantry
Ginn, J.J., Private, Company F, 57th Indiana Infantry
Morrell, O.O., Private, Company H, 57th Indiana Infantry
Smith, F.J., Private, Company H, 57th Indiana Infantry
Hackinsberg, A., Private, Company I, 57th Indiana Infantry
Norris, Daniel, Private, Company I, 57th Indiana Infantry
Gardner, J.W., Private, Company B, 65th Indiana Infantry
Dickey, J.K., Private, Company K, 65th Indiana Infantry
Mulligan, T.W., Sergeant, Company G, 65th Indiana Infantry
Elliott, D., Private, Company E, 75th Indiana Infantry
Medsher, Private, Company A, 79th Indiana Infantry
Winkless, S., Private, Company B, 79th Indiana Infantry
Chapel, Issac, Private, Company C, 79th Indiana Infantry
West, E., Private, Company E, 79th Indiana Infantry
Dixon, G., Private, Company C, 80th Indiana Infantry
Hashawe, A., Private, Company C, 80th Indiana Infantry
Rawley, Jno., Private, Company C, 80th Indiana Infantry
Reynolds, M., Private, Company C, 80th Indiana Infantry
Runkle, M., Private, Company C, 80th Indiana Infantry
Summerson, Private, Company C, 80th Indiana Infantry
Naler, T.H., Private, Company K, 84th Indiana Infantry
Hogrlin, Jas., Sergeant, Company C, 84th Indiana Infantry
Lawrence, H.K., Corporal, Company H, 88th Indiana Infantry
Phince, Corporal, Company A, 89th Indiana Infantry
Habbier, H., Private, Company G, 91st Indiana Infantry
Willard, C., Private, Company E., 92nd Indiana Infantry
Lidy, Sam, Private, Company A, 93rd Indiana Infantry
Peterson, Mat., Private, Company A, 93rd Indiana Infantry
Penster, J., Corporal, Company B, 93rd Indiana Infantry
Franklin, M.S., Private, Company C, 93rd Indiana Infantry
Garnett, J., Private, Company C, 93rd Indiana Infantry
Pettrits, D., Private, Company C, 93rd Indiana Infantry
Grove, Jas., Private, Company D, 93rd Indiana Infantry
Buchanan, Wm., Private, Company D, 93rd Indiana Infantry

McGinnis, Jno., Private, Company E, 93rd Indiana Infantry
Stockdale, L., Private, Company E, 93rd Indiana Infantry
Alton, R., Private, Company F, 93rd Indiana Infantry
Gass, N.J., Sergeant, Company H, 93rd Indiana Infantry
Young, J., Private, Company L, 93rd Indiana Infantry
Alexander, J.C., Private, Company C, 98th Indiana Infantry
Gilmore, J., Private, Company E, 93rd Indiana Infantry
Higgins, E.E., Private, Company I, 93rd Indiana Infantry
Cass, J.W., Private, Company B, 99th Indiana Infantry
Van Over, J., Private, Company C, 99th Indiana Infantry
Rodgers, T., Private, Company G, 99th Indiana Infantry
York, A.J., Private, Company G, 99th Indiana Infantry
Lindlay, H.C., Private, Company I, 99th Indiana Infantry
Moreh, H.O., Sergeant, Company K, 99th Indiana Infantry
Noss, J.A., Private, Company B, 101st Indiana Infantry
Morter, J.A., Private, Company C, 124th Indiana Infantry
Pain, J., Private, Company C, 124th Indiana Infantry
Thompson, J.W., Private, Company C, 124th Indiana Infantry
Brown, Jas., Private, Company C, 124th Indiana Infantry
Bryant, C., Private, Company C, 124th Indiana Infantry
Johan, Jas., Private, Company C, 124th Indiana Infantry
Shinnyfield, S., Private, Company C, 124th Indiana Infantry
White, T.A., Private, Company C, 124th Indiana Infantry
Elliott, Jas., Private, Company I, 124th Indiana Infantry
Kimperlain, J.H., Sergeant, Company K, 124th Indiana Infantry
Herrington, P., Private, Company K, 124th Indiana Infantry
Palmer, R., Private, Company K, 124th Indiana Infantry
Beardon, D.S., Corporal, Company C, 124th Indiana Infantry
Esby, J.M., Corporal, Company C, 124th Indiana Infantry
Hickerson, J.A., Corporal, Company C, 124th Indiana Infantry
Raymond, W.H., Corporal, Company C, 124th Indiana Infantry
Wright, J.C., Corporal, 124th Indiana Infantry
Dowhar, L., Private, Company C, 124th Indiana Infantry
Meher, D., Musician, Company I, 124th Indiana Infantry
Cox, W.H., Private, Company B, 1st Kentucky Cavalry

Cummings, C., Private, Company I, 1st Kentucky Cavalry
Marshall, J.T., Private, Company C, 2nd Kentucky Cavalry
Cook, W.H.H., Corporal, Company E, 2nd Kentucky Cavalry
Hall, R.T., Private, Company K, 2nd Kentucky Cavalry
Banks, J.N., Private, Company A, 3rd Kentucky Cavalry
Marslin, F., Private, Company B, 3rd Kentucky Cavalry
Ballard, Private, Company F, 3rd Kentucky Cavalry
Winhasher, J., Private, Company G, 3rd Kentucky Cavalry
Gray, S., Private, Company A, 4th Kentucky Cavalry
Johnson, W., Private, Company A, 4th Kentucky Cavalry
Royalty, D.B., Private, Company A, 4th Kentucky Cavalry
Bende, N., Private, Company B, 4th Kentucky Cavalry
Beckett, B., Private, Company B, 4th Kentucky Cavalry
Foods, A.H., Private, Company B, 4th Kentucky Cavalry
Marcum, N., Private, Company B, 4th Kentucky Cavalry
Carey, J., Sergeant, Company C, 4th Kentucky Cavalry
Spencer, A., Sergeant, Company C, 4th Kentucky Cavalry
Bowland, Abner, Private, Company C, 4th Kentucky Cavalry
Higdon, E.T., Private, Company C, 4th Kentucky Cavalry
McQueen, A., Private, Company D, 4th Kentucky Cavalry
Gallagher, J., Private, Company D, 4th Kentucky Cavalry
Papers, J., Private, Company E, 4th Kentucky Cavalry
Bower, M., Private, Company F, 4th Kentucky Cavalry
Harper, E., Private, Company G, 4th Kentucky Cavalry
Jackson, G., Private, Company G, 4th Kentucky Cavalry
Hogan, M., Private, Company H, 4th Kentucky Cavalry
Holley, J.W., Private, Company H, 4th Kentucky Cavalry
Vincent, H., Private, Company H, 4th Kentucky Cavalry
Redman, W., Private, Company H, 4th Kentucky Cavalry
Curry, M., Private, Company I, 4th Kentucky Cavalry
Galiner, James, Private, Company I, 4th Kentucky Cavalry
Regney, James, Private, Company I, 4th Kentucky Cavalry
Csuleter, M., Private, Company K, 4th Kentucky Cavalry
Edwards, W. H., Private, Company K, 4th Kentucky Cavalry
Fabrow, M.B., Private, Company K, 4th Kentucky Cavalry

Merrell, F., Private, Company K, 4th Kentucky Cavalry
Williams, W.T., Private, Company K, 4th Kentucky Cavalry
Wolum, Jno., Private, Company K, 4th Kentucky Cavalry
Collins, Wm., Private, Company L, 4th Kentucky Cavalry
Patterson, Thos., Private, Company L, 4th Kentucky Cavalry
Fiddler, W.N., Major, 5th Kentucky Cavalry
Faber, J.H., Private, Company A, 5th Kentucky Cavalry
Wheatleigh, L., Sergeant, Company A, 6th Kentucky Cavalry
Bankhead, Henry, Private, Company A, 6th Kentucky Cavalry
Hammond, Jno., Private, Company A, 6th Kentucky Cavalry
Beam, L., Private, Company A, 6th Kentucky Cavalry
Haup, Benj., Private, Company A, 6th Kentucky Cavalry
McKrunney, R., Private, Company A, 6th Kentucky Cavalry
Hartman, L., Private, Company B, 6th Kentucky Cavalry
Lebel, G., Private, Company B, 6th Kentucky Cavalry
Stewart, P.A., Private, Company B, 6th Kentucky Cavalry
Parish, C.H., Captain, Company C, 6th Kentucky Cavalry
Fluke, A.W., Sergeant, Company C, 6th Kentucky Cavalry
Root, E., Sergeant, Company C, 6th Kentucky Cavalry
Firey, J., Bugler, Company C, 6th Kentucky Cavalry
Buckley, Jas., Private, Company C, 6th Kentucky Cavalry
Barlett, C.M., Private, Company C, 6th Kentucky Cavalry
Coleman, E., Private, Company C, 6th Kentucky Cavalry
Elliott, W., Private, Company C, 6th Kentucky Cavalry
Merrit, B., Private, Company C, 6th Kentucky Cavalry
Moprin, T., Private, Company C, 6th Kentucky Cavalry
Paller, W., Private, Company C, 6th Kentucky Cavalry
Pierce, W., Private, Company C, 6th Kentucky Cavalry
Watt, J.S., Private, Company C, 6th Kentucky Cavalry
Vanor, W.D., Private, Company C, 6th Kentucky Cavalry
Allison, R.C., Private, Company D, 6th Kentucky Cavalry
Cuney, E.C., Private, Company D, 6th Kentucky Cavalry
Evensberry, H., Private, Company E, 6th Kentucky Cavalry
Calvin, J., Private, Company F, 6th Kentucky Cavalry
Calvin, W.L., Private, Company F, 6th Kentucky Cavalry

Carmarch, J., Private, Company F, 6th Kentucky Cavalry
Cheatham, G.H., Private, Company F, 6th Kentucky Cavalry
Saber, J.J., 1st Lieutenant, Company G, 6th Kentucky Cavalry
Chelf, S.D., Corporal, Company G, 6th Kentucky Cavalry
Stherher, T.J., Atrificer, Company G, 6th Kentucky Cavalry
Brown, P.M., Private, Company G, 6th Kentucky Cavalry
Davenport, Seth, Private, Company G, 6th Kentucky Cavalry
Jacobs, A.M., Private, Company G, 6th Kentucky Cavalry
Jacobs, J.A., Private, Company G, 6th Kentucky Cavalry
Hobbs, L., Private, Company G, 6th Kentucky Cavalry
Lay, G.W., Private, Company G, 6th Kentucky Cavalry
Monday, W.H., Private, Company G, 6th Kentucky Cavalry
Noe, H.H., Private, Company G, 6th Kentucky Cavalry
Saddler, M., Private, Company G, 6th Kentucky Cavalry
Stephens, T.N., Private, Company G, 6th Kentucky Cavalry
Winstead, Jno., Private, Company G, 6th Kentucky Cavalry
Daugherty, Thos., Private, Company H, 6th Kentucky Cavalry
Hoglyn, J.B., Private, Company H, 6th Kentucky Cavalry
Thompson, J.B., Private, Company H, 6th Kentucky Cavalry
Carter, T.A., Private, Company A, 17th Kentucky Cavalry
Wade, Jas., Private, Company B, 27th Kentucky Cavalry
Smith, Jas., Private, Company D, 27th Kentucky Cavalry
Clark, M.C., Sergeant, Company B, 28th Kentucky Cavalry
Foley, P.W., Corporal, Company B, 28th Kentucky Cavalry
Cook, J., Private, Company A, 1st Kentucky Artillery
Lewis, W., Corporal, Company H, 1st Kentucky Artillery
Phelps, J.W., Private, Company G, 4th Kentucky Mt'd Infantry
Arnold, W.F., Corporal, Company B, 1st Kentucky Infanrty
Miller, R., Private, Company K, 1st Kentucky Infantry
Johnson, A.W., Private, Company H, 2nd Kentucky Infantry
Penticuff, Jno., Private, Company A, 3rd Kentucky Infantry
Barrow, G.E., Private, Company D, 3rd Kentucky Infantry
Wallace, F., Private, Company D, 3rd Kentucky Infantry
Elmor, R., Private, Company G, 3rd Kentucky Infantry
Raysor, W., Private, Company H, 3rd Kentucky Infantry

Hope, F.W., Private, Company A, 4th Kentucky Infantry
Gillman, H., Private, Company C, 4th Kentucky Infantry
Humphreys, B., Private, Company H, 4th Kentucky Infantry
Webster, P., Private, Company E, 4th Kentucky Infantry
Kennedy, E.R., Private, Company K, Kentucky Infantry
Baxon, Jno., Private, Company B, 5th Kentucky Infantry
Hagart, W., Private, Company A, 7th Kentucky Cavalry
Coyton, W.A., Private, Company B, 7th Kentucky Cavalry
Davis, B.G., Private, Company L, 7th Kentucky Cavalry
Smith, J., Private, Company G, 11th Kentucky Infantry
Clinger, C., Corporal, Company E, 16th Kentucky Infantry
Wilson, H.B., Corporal, Company E, 16th Kentucky Infantry
Emerick, J., Private, Company L, 18th Kentucky Infantry
Smith, C., Private, Company D, 27th Kentucky Infantry
Neller, Peter, Private, Company C, 28th Kentucky Infantry
Colwell, H.C., Company D, 37th Kentucky Infantry
Free, M.C., Private, Company M, 1st Michigan Cavalry
Watson, J.H., Private, Company M, 1st Michigan Cavalry
Paelps, F., Private, Company M, 1st Michigan Cavalry
Dickerson, Simeon, Lieutenant, Co. E, 2nd Michigan Cavalry
Maxon, M., Sergeant, Company A, 2nd Michigan Cavalry
Alfred, Z., Private, Company A, 2nd Michigan Cavalry
Johnson, B., Private, Company A, 2nd Michigan Cavalry
Tubbs, Hiram, Private, Company B, 2nd Michigan Cavalry
Brooks, L., Sergeant, Company C, 2nd Michigan Cavalry
Robinson, J.L., Private, Company C, 2nd Michigan Cavalry
Corliss, J. L., Private, Company C, 2nd Michigan Cavalry
Dillard, James, Private, Company C, 2nd Michigan Cavalry
Gleason, G.G., Private, Company D, 2nd Michigan Cavalry
Johnson, J., Private, Company D, 2nd Michigan Cavalry
Hill, Daniel, Private, Company D, 2nd Michigan Cavalry
Dickens, L.F., Lieutenant, Company E, 2nd Michigan Cavalry
Perkins, F.M., Sergeant, Company E, 2nd Michigan Cavalry
Petitt, M., Corporal, Company E, 2nd Michigan Cavalry
Warren, D. Private, Company E, 2nd Michigan Cavalry

Nolen, D., Private, Company E, 2nd Michigan Cavalry
Munroe, F., Private, Company E, 2nd Michigan Cavalry
Scadding, J., Private, Company E, 2nd Michigan Cavalry
Alney, John, Private, Company E, 2nd Michigan Cavalry
Draiman, McKenzie, Private, Co. E, 2nd Michigan Cavalry
Thomas, J.P., Private, Company E, 2nd Michigan Cavalry
Kendric, J., Private, Company E, 2nd Michigan Cavalry
Langley, W., Private, Company E, 2nd Michigan Cavalry
Lindsay, W.L., Private, Company E, 2nd Michigan Cavalry
Byron, Joseph, Private, Company E, 2nd Michigan Cavalry
Rix, A., Private, Company G, 2nd Michigan Cavalry
Worden, D.C., Bugler, Company H, 2nd Michigan Cavalry
Holler, R., Private, Company H, 2nd Michigan Cavalry
Mahony, J., Corporal, Company I, 2nd Michigan Cavalry
Gage, G., Private, Company I, 2nd Michigan Cavalry
Barker, F., Private, Company K, 2nd Michigan Cavalry
Stranton, L., Private, Company K, 2nd Michigan Cavalry
Cormstead, Private, Company K, 2nd Michigan Cavalry
Laybarker, P., Corporal, Company L, 2nd Michigan Cavalry
Ranks, F., Private, Company D, 3rd Michigan Cavalry
Thompson, M., Company I, 3rd Michigan Cavalry
Baker, M.S., Corporal, Company D, 4th Michigan Cavalry
Blakely, J., Private, Company E, 4th Michigan Cavalry
Eslich, N.A., Private, Company G, 4th Michigan Cavalry
Davenhaff, J.C., Private, Company I, 4th Michigan Cavalry
Fordend, L.D., Private, Company I, 4th Michigan, Cavalry
Norton, J.E., Private, Company I, 4th Michigan Cavalry
Finch, Wm., Private, Company D, 5th Michigan Cavalry
Warren, H., Sergeant, Company G, Michigan Cavalry
Russell, A., Private, Company G, 5th Michigan Cavalry
Cehart, J.L., Sergeant, Company H, 5th Michigan Cavalry
Brown, J.W., Private, Company H, 5th Michigan Cavalry
Bussley, L., Private, Company M, 5th Michigan Cavalry
Barnes, A.M., Private, Company D, 6th Michigan Cavalry
Pick, C., Private, Company E, 6th Michigan Cavalry

Morse, V.H., Private, Company E, 6th Michigan Cavalry
Hart, T., Private, Company I, 6th Michigan Cavalry
Hulett, J., Private, Company K, 6th Michigan Cavalry
McNeal, B., Private, Company H, 7th Michigan Cavalry
Zachary, A.K., Sergeant, Company K, 7th Michigan Cavalry
Noble, John, Private, Company B, 8th Michigan Cavalry
Lebrey, C.J., Private, Company B, 8th Michigan Cavalry
Fast, L.R., Private, Company B, 8th Michigan Cavalry
Glum, T.P., Sergeant, Company C, 8th Michigan Cavalry
Fritzgerald, W., Private, Company C, 8th Michigan Cavalry
Snyder, H., Private, Company C, 8th Michigan Cavalry
Vent, W., Private, Company C, 8th Michigan Cavalry
Duberry, A., Private, Company D, 8th Michigan Cavalry
Wells, H.C., Sergeant, Company E, 8th Michigan Cavalry
Geer, C.B., Private, Company F, 8th Michigan Cavalry
Warls, B., Private, Company G, 8th Michigan Cavalry
Lubustacker, Private, Company G, 8th Michigan Cavalry
Meeker, Clark, Private, Company H, 8th Michigan Cavalry
Smith, Freeman, Private, Company H, 8th Michigan Cavalry
Snider, T., Private, Company H, 8th Michigan Cavalry
Spencer, E., Private, Company H, 8th Michigan Cavalry
Burlingham, E.J., Private, Company I, 8th Michigan Cavalry
Carey, O., Private, Company I, 8th Michigan Cavalry
Cartwright, Private, Company I, 8th Michigan Cavalry
Farrer, John, Private, Company K, 8th Michigan Cavalry
Day, J.P., Corporal, Company L, 8th Michigan Cavalry
Broadshaw, D., Private, Company M, 8th Michigan Cavalry
Zacharia, M., Private, Company M, 8th Michigan Cavalry
Patterson, W.J., 1st Lieutenant, Co. E, 9th Michigan Cavalry
Wells, D.A., Private, Company E, 1st Michigan S.S.
Green, A., Private, Company K, 1st Michigan S.S.
Royal, L.S., Private, Company K, 1st Michigan S.S.
Hatch, A.W., Corporal, Company F, 1st Michigan E & M
Bremer, J.L., Sergeant, Company L, 1st Michigan E & M
Earl, J., Lieutenant, Company L, 1st Michigan E & M

Johnson, H., Private, Company L, 1st Michigan E & M
Decker, J.R., Private, Company L, 1st Michigan E & M
Stephens, J.A., Sergeant, Company B, 1st Michigan Infantry
Shepard, S., Private, Company D, 1st Michigan Infantry
Ives, E.H., Private, Company D, 1st Michigan Infantry
Barr, G., Private, Company G, 11th Michigan Infantry
Butler, J.E., Private, Company A, 15th Michigan Infantry
Wads, A., Private, Company A, 15th Michigan Infantry
Ducatt, T.A., Corporal, Company E, 15th Michigan Infantry
Wright, H., Private, Company F, 15th Michigan Infantry
Wells, W., Private, Company H, 15th Michigan Infantry
Doane, F.R., Private, Company B, 17th Michigan Infantry
Peacham, T.J., Corporal, Company F, 17th Michigan Infantry
Waterbury, A.N., Sergeant, Company H, 17th Michigan
Briggs, J.C., Sergeant, Company K, 17th Michigan Infantry
Spring, J., Corporal, Company A, 18th Michigan Infantry
Knapp, A.J., Corporal, Company A, 18th Michigan Infantry
Bradish, J., Corporal, Company A, 18th Michigan Infantry
Johnson, G.J., Private Company A, 18th Michigan Infantry
Prosser, G.W., Private, Company A, 18th Michigan Infantry
Doney, N., Private, Company A, 18th Michigan Infantry
Foglesong, N., Private, Company A, 18th Michigan Infantry
Koon, H., Private, Company A, 18th Michigan Infantry
Myers, J.L., Private, Company A, 18th Michigan Infantry
Robbins, J., Private, Company A, 18th Michigan Infantry
Rowley, O.B., Private, Company A, 18th Michigan Infantry
Slick, J.L., Private, Company A, 18th Michigan Infantry
Ludlum, E.F., Private, Company A, 18th Michigan Infantry
Hale, O.P., Private, Company A, 18th Michigan Infantry
Rowley, W., Private, Company A, 18th Michigan Infantry
Cornell, A.W., Corporal, Company B, 18th Michigan Infantry
Aldrich, A.D., Private, Company B, 18th Michigan Infantry
Darrow, S.M., Private, Company B, 18th Michigan Infantry
Wright, F., Sergeant, Company B, 18th Michigan Infantry
Ainsworth, J.S., Private, Company B 18th Michigan Infantry

Sprague, F., Private, Company B, 18th Michigan Infantry
Horton, C.F., Sergeant, Company C, 18th Michigan Infantry
Greenfield, L., Sergeant, Company C, 18th Michigan Infantry
Baker, J.D., 1st Sergeant, Company C, 18th Michigan Infantry
Moore, J., Corporal, Company C, 18th Michigan Infantry
Thayer, Wm., Private, Company C, 18th Michigan Infantry
Oakley, E.J., Private, Company C, 18th Michigan Infantry
Zidler, F., Private, Company C, 18th Michigan Infantry
Deline, O., Private, Company C, 18th Michigan Infantry
Daly, M., Private, Company C, 18th Michigan Infantry
Southwick, E., Private, Company C, 18th Michigan Infantry
Hayck, G.P., Private, Company C, 18th Michigan Infantry
Parker, J., Private, Company C, 18th Michigan Infantry
Potter, J.B., Private, Company C, 18th Michigan Infantry
Finch, W.H., Sergeant, Company D, 18th Michigan Infantry
Lawrence, Albert, Sergeant, Co. D, 18th Michigan Infantry
Wood, H.C., Corporal, Company D, 18th Michigan Infantry
Ford, E., Corporal, Company D, 18th Michigan Infantry
Young, W., Musician, Company D, 18th Michigan Infantry
Mann, W., Private, Company D, 18th Michigan Infantry
Nelson, L., Private, Company D, 18th Michigan Infantry
Crisp, Wm., Private, Company D, 18th Michigan Infantry
Norcutt, J.W., Private, Company D, 18th Michigan Infantry
Duesler, Geo., Private, Company D, 18th Michigan Infantry
Vancourt, J., Private, Company D, 18th Michigan Infantry
Walkins, J., Private, Company D, 18th Michigan Infantry
Wright, N.D., Private, Company D, 18th Michigan Infantry
Eddy, W., Private, Company D, 18th Michigan Infantry
Bird, John, Private, Company D, 18th Michigan Infantry
Robins, Jonathan, Private, Company D, 18th Michigan Infantry
Brewer, G.H., Corporal, Company E, 18th Michigan Infantry
Jones, S.W., Private, Company E, 18th Michigan Infantry
Brangan, P., Private, Company E, 18th Michigan Infantry
Millspaugh, D., Private, Company E, 18th Michigan Infantry
Barnum, J.P., Private, Company E, 18th Michigan Infantry

Randall, A., Private, Company E, 18th Michigan Infantry
Randall, A., Private, Company E, 18th Michigan Infantry
Smith, Thos., Private, Company E, 18th Michigan Infantry
Mason, G.R., Private, Company E, 18th Michigan Infantry
Goodrich, U.N., Private, Company E, 18th Michigan Infantry
Voglesong, A.N., Sergeant, Co. F, 18th Michigan Infantry
Cole, O.M., Corporal, Company F, 18th Michigan Infantry
Stubberfield, W., Private, Company F, 18th Michigan Infantry
Harris, W.H., Private, Company F, 18th Michigan Infantry
Holmes, N.L., Private, Company F, 18th Michigan Infantry
Vangorder, D.W., Private, Company F, 18th Michigan Infantry
Smith, C., Private, Company F, 18th Michigan Infantry
Abbadusky, C., Private, Company F, 18th Michigan Infantry
Gale, A. (Orris), Private, Company F, 18th Michigan Infantry
Vanvlack, A., Private, Company F., 18th Michigan Infantry
Fuller, A., Private, Company F, 18th Michigan Infantry
Hines, T.F., Private, Company K, 18th Michigan Infantry
Hampton, F., Private, Company G, 18th Michigan Infantry
Williams, W.H., Private, Company F, 18th Michigan Infantry
Nevins, J.F., Private, Company F, 18th Michigan Infantry
Lachler, Geo., Private, Company F, 18th Michigan Infantry
Palmer, G.N., Corporal, Company G, 18th Michigan Infantry
Faurot, W.L., Corporal, Company G, 18th Michigan Infantry
Lackey, P., Private, Company G, 18th Michigan Infantry
Hampton, P., Private, Company G, 18th Michigan Infantry
Burns, E., Private, Company G, 18th Michigan Infantry
Burns, M., Private, Company G, 18th Michigan Infantry
Merrifield, E.C., Private, Company G, 18th Michigan Infantry
Colwell, James, Private, Company G, 18th Michigan Infantry
Seely, F.D., Private, Company G, 18th Michigan Infantry
Plank, H.D., Corporal, Company H, 18th Michigan Infantry
Countryman, G.A., Musician, Co. K, 18th Michigan Infantry
Haight, G.C., Musician, Company H, 18th Michigan Infantry
Mallison, S., Private, Company H, 18th Michigan Infantry
Fink, M.L., Private, Company H, 18th Michigan Infantry
Snyder, D.L., Private, Company H, 18th Michigan Infantry

Shaffer, B.B., Private, Company I, 18th Michigan Infantry

Main, S.H., Private, Company I, 18th Michigan Infantry

Patterson, R., Private, Company I, 18th Michigan Infantry

Upton, W.S., Private, Company I, 18th Michigan Infantry

Wiechard, A.B., Private Company K, 18th Michigan Infantry

Sulier, L.C., Private, Company K, 18th Michigan Infantry

Shetterson, Jno., Private, Company K, 18th Michigan Infantry

McEldowney, A.J., Private, Co. K, 18th Michigan Infantry

Berry, C.D., Private, Company I, 20th Michigan Infantry

Mead, J., Private, Company F, 21st Michigan Infantry

Seward, R.W., Private, Company F, 21st Michigan Infantry

Love, J.H., Private, Company C, 22nd Michigan Infantry

Smith, A.B., Sergeant, Company K, 22nd Michigan Infantry

Boyce, E., Private, Company K, 22nd Michigan Infantry

Cole, David, Private, Company B, 23rd Michigan Infantry

Freeland, G., Private, Company E, 23rd Michigan Infantry

Ludlow, A.F., Private, Company E, 23rd Michigan Infantry

Westhorpe, Geo., Private, Company E, 23rd Michigan Infantry

Vancover, A., Private, Company E, 23rd Michigan Infantry

Harris, Israel, Private, Company H, 24th Michigan Infantry

Luchane, D., Private, Company F, 25th Michigan Infantry

Bement, Geo., Sergeant, Company F, 25th Michigan Infantry

Richardson, T.W., Private, Company A, 1st Ohio Infantry

Banner, Thos., Private, Company B, 1st Ohio Infantry

Anderson, James, Private, Company D, 1st Ohio Infantry

Eavens, E., Private, Company D, 1st Ohio Infantry

Hawk, M., Private, Company D, 3rd Ohio Infantry

Sorger, G., Private, Company G, 4th Ohio Infantry

Edwards, Jacob, Private, Company I, 4th Ohio Infantry

Lentimore, J.B., Private, Company M, 4th Ohio Infantry

Madden, W.P., Private, Company L, 8th Ohio Infantry

Miller, D.S., Private, Company D, 13th Ohio Infantry

Longshon, J., Private, Company I, 13th Ohio Infantry

McCordy, I., Private, Company K, 13th Ohio Infantry

Nelson, N., Private, Company K, 13th Ohio Infantry

Van Fleet, H., Private, Company I, 14th Ohio Infantry
Carter, F.M., Private, Company D, 15th Ohio Infantry
Ezzle, M., Private, Company F, 15th Ohio Infantry
Myers, C.W., Private, Company G, 15th Ohio Infantry
Carnes, N., Sergeant, Company B, 18th Ohio Infantry
Lampsell, H., Private, 11th Ohio Infantry
White, W.A., Private, Company H, 19th Ohio Infantry
Shirley, W.H., Sergeant, Company B, 21st Ohio Infantry
Casbell, A., Private, Company B, 21st Ohio Infantry
Markford, P., Private, Company B, 21st Ohio Infantry
Morgan, Levi, Private, Company B, 21st Ohio Infantry
Usher, A., Private, Company B, 21st Ohio Infantry
Engal, J., Private, Company D, 21st Ohio Infantry
Donaphin, A., Sergeant, Company E, Ohio Infantry
Kendals, R., Private, Company E, 21st Ohio Infantry
Forest, F., Private, Company K, 21st Ohio Infantry
Davidson, John, Private, Company A, 22nd Ohio Infantry
Mershen, G., Private, Company E, 22nd Ohio Infantry
Field, G.G., Corporal, Company D, 23rd Ohio Infantry
Gray, William, Private, Company L, 23rd Ohio Infantry
Babcock, John, Private, Company K, 24th Ohio Infantry
Kelly, J., Private, Company K, 25th Ohio Infantry
Miller, J.R., Corporal, Company D, 26th Ohio Infantry
McClutock, W.G., Private, Company H, 26th Ohio Infantry
Sheilds, P., Private, Company D, 31st Ohio Infantry
Long, J.B., Private, Company I, 33rd Ohio Infantry
Lyman, R.J., Private, Company I, 33rd Ohio Infantry
Sheppard, W., Private, Company E, 34th Ohio Infantry
Whyler, L., Private, Company D, 35th Ohio Infantry
Sharp, E., Private, Company E, 35th Ohio Infantry
Brown, A., Private, Company A, 37th Ohio Infantry
Wertermier, J.D., Private, Company B, 37th Ohio Infantry
Anderback, G., Private, Company C, 37th Ohio Infantry
Webler, John, Private, Company C, 37th Ohio Infantry
Cealer, C., Private, Company D, 37th Ohio Infantry

Hysenger, J., Private, Company D, 37th Ohio Infantry
Hiss, John, Private, Company E, 37th Ohio Infantry
Mathews, O., Private, Company D, 41st Ohio Infantry
Clearley, J.R., Private, Company F, 41st Ohio Infantry
Shacher, J., Private, Company E, 42nd Ohio Infantry
Thacker, J., Private, Company D, 46th Ohio Infantry
Klutter, L.R., Private, Company K, 46th Ohio Infantry
Mass, J.W., Private, Company B, 47th Ohio Infantry
Buckleyhower, A., Company H, 47th Ohio Infantry
Hesser, L., Private, Company K, 47th Ohio Infantry
Gay, Asa, Private, Company A, 49th Ohio Infantry
Huffey, J., Private, Company B, 49th Ohio Infantry
Fox, John, Corporal, Company A, 50th Ohio Infantry
Rice, M.L., Private, Company A, 50th Ohio Infantry
Roberts, Jno., Private, Company A, 50th Ohio Infantry
Hellinger, J., Sergeant, Company B, 50th Ohio Infantry
Humphrey, W.C., Private, Company B, 50th Ohio Infantry
Merron, William, Private, Company B, 50th Ohio Infantry
Sheare, W.G., Private, Company B, 50th Ohio Infantry
Walker, J., Private, Company B, 50th Ohio Infantry
Huston, D., Corporal, Company C, 50th Ohio Infantry
Ray, Christian, Private, Company C, 50th Ohio Infantry
Picket, E., Corporal, Company D, 50th Ohio Infantry
McClearly, Private, Company D, 50th Ohio Infantry
Holmes, S., Private, Company D, 50th Ohio Infantry
Richmond, W., Private, Company D, 50th Ohio Infantry
Shulton, William, Private, Company D, 50th Ohio Infantry
White, G.W., Private, Company D, 50th Ohio Infantry
Lee, William H., Sergeant, Company E, 50th Ohio Infantry
Ruslant, Peter, Corporal, Company E, 50th Ohio Infantry
Vananda, R., Corporal, Company E, 50th Ohio Infantry
Carr, John, Private, Company E, 50th Ohio Infantry
Krinzer, H., Private, Company E, 50th Ohio Infantry
Meaker, F., Private, Company E, 50th Ohio Infantry
Pettyjohn, S., Private, Company E, 50th Ohio Infantry

Moore, T., Private, Company F, 50th Ohio Infantry
Green, W., Sergeant, Company G, 50th Ohio Infantry
Cruse, C. F., Corporal Company G, 50th Ohio Infantry
Bacan, Nornear, Private, Company G, 50th Ohio Infantry
Badgley, B.B., Private, Company G, 50th Ohio Infantry
Boyd, George W., Private, Company G, 50th Ohio Infantry
Cotton, W.S., Private, Company G, 50th Ohio Infantry
Lehman, N., Private, Company G, 50th Ohio Infantry
Station, G.W., Private, Company G, 50th Ohio Infantry
Gilmore, S.D., Private, Company H, 50th Ohio Infantry
Griffin, J.O., Private, Company H, 50th Ohio Infantry
Jordon, H., Private, Company H, 50th Ohio Infantry
Matter, F., Private, Company H, 50th Ohio Infantry
Murphy, C.C., Private, Company H, 50th Ohio Infantry
Winters, Corporal, Company K, 50th Ohio Infantry
Shellard, P., Private, Company K, 50th Ohio Infantry
Culp, A.J., Private, Company K, 50th Ohio Infantry
Philips, W., Private, Company B, 51st Ohio Infantry
Norris, J.B., Private, Company C, 51st Ohio Infantry
DeMoss, J., Private, Company D, 51st Ohio Infantry
Smith, W., Private, Company D, 51st Ohio Infantry
Altof, E.W., Private, Company E, 51st Ohio Infantry
Belnap, C.M., Private, Company F, 51st Ohio Infantry
Lahr, J., Private, Company F, 51st Ohio Infantry
Sayer, S.R., Sergeant, Company H, 51st Ohio Infantry
Hleg, L., Corporal, Company I, 51st Ohio Infantry
Miller, J., Private, Company E, 52nd Ohio Infantry
Gregery, W., Private, Company C, 53rd Ohio Infantry
Scan, W., Private, Company C, 54th Ohio Infantry
Patte, W.S., Private, Company G, 54th Ohio Infantry
Wiles, A.G., Private, Company C, 55th Ohio Infantry
Githorn, L., Private, Company F, 56th Ohio Infantry
Blaire, P.Q., Q'Master Sgt., 59th Ohio Infantry
Brumer, M., Private, Company C, 59th Ohio Infantry
Brudgeman, A.A, Private, Company F, 63rd Ohio Infantry

Whoyle, L., Sergeant, Company G, 63rd Ohio Infantry

Barnes, W., Private, Company H, 63rd Ohio Infantry

Hult, W.A., Corporal, Company A, 64th Ohio Infantry

Van Scoyte, G.W., Corporal, Company A, 64th Ohio Infantry

Brinke, Thos., Private, Company A, 64th Ohio Infantry

Fise, W., Sergeant, Company B, 64th Ohio Infantry

Cramer, A.O., Sergeant, Company B, 64th Ohio Infantry

Barr, W., Private, Company B, 64th Ohio Infantry

Brady, J., Private, Company B, 64th Ohio Infantry

King, B., Private, Company B, 64th Ohio Infantry

Zummer, C., Private, Company B, 64th Ohio Infantry

Zimmer, C., Private, Company B, 64th Ohio Infantry

Benton, H.W., Sergeant, Company D, 64th Ohio Infantry

Landon, S., Corporal, Company D, 64th Ohio Infantry

Carnock, T.J., Corporal, Company E, 64th Ohio Infantry

White, R., Sergeant, Company I, 64th Ohio Infantry

Eddermon, D., Corporal, Company I, 64th Ohio Infantry

McKinley, D., Private, Company I, 64th Ohio Infantry

Stickney, J., Private, Company I, 64th Ohio Infantry

Kennedy, Ed, Private, Company K, 64th Ohio Infantry

Ryan, J., Private, Company K, 64th Ohio Infantry

Gregory, E., Sergeant, Company C, 65th Ohio Infantry

Nickerson, Chas., Private, Company E, 65th Ohio Infantry

Grebaugh, D., Private, Company G, 65th Ohio Infantry

Mathias, E., Sergeant, Company K, 65th Ohio Infantry

Horner, Ira B., Corporal, Company K, 65th Ohio Infantry

Bishler, Jno., Private, Company K, 65th Ohio Infantry

Emerlin, Eli, Private, Company K, 65th Ohio Infantry

Fairchild, O.W., Private, Company K, 65th Ohio Infantry

Roddybaugh, S.H., Company K, 65th Ohio Infantry

Shoemaker, J., Private, Company C, 70th Ohio Infantry

Black, J.C., Private, Company K, 70th Ohio Infantry

Davis, J.W., Lieutenant, Company B, 71st Ohio Infantry

Brant, F., Private, Company A, 72nd Ohio Infantry

McIntyre, B., Private, Company B, 72nd Ohio Infantry

Shoe, E., Private, Company C, 72nd Ohio Infantry
Duke, Wm., Sergeant, Company D, 72nd Ohio Infantry
Stalley, M., Sergeant, Company D, 72nd Ohio Infantry
Shoemaker, A., Private, Company E, 72nd Ohio Infantry
Shoemaker, W., Private, Company E, 72nd Ohio Infantry
Trimmer, Wm., Private, Company E, 72nd Ohio Infantry
Flint, Thos., Corporal, Company F, 72nd Ohio Infantry
Crane, J., Private, Company F, 72nd Ohio Infantry
Hague, S., Private, Company F, 72nd Ohio Infantry
Kirk, W. H., Private, Company F, 72nd Ohio Infantry
Aubrey, Private, Company H, 72nd Ohio Infantry
Holendesk, J., Private, Company K, 72nd Ohio Infantry
Andrews, W., Sergeant, Company A, 75th Ohio Infantry
Barnes, Ed., Private, Company F, 75th Ohio Infantry
Waltz, M., Private, Company H, 75th Ohio Infantry
Thompson, J., Private, Company A, 76th Ohio Infantry
Yeisley, E.H., Private, Company A, 76th Ohio Infantry
McCarty, Jas., Private, Company D, 76th Ohio Infantry
Stone, Jas., Private, Company D, 76th Ohio Infantry
Thomas, Thos., Private, Company H, 76th Ohio Infantry
White, Jas., Private, Company E, 78th Ohio Infantry
Clepner, J., Private, Company H, 78th Ohio Infantry
Marks, Chas., Private, Company F, 79th Ohio Infantry
Rammel, A.W., Private, Company E, 80th Ohio Infantry
Shaw, C.M., Private, Company B, 81st Ohio Infantry
Cord, A., Private, Company F, 90th Ohio Infantry
Nihart, A., Private, Company G, 90th Ohio Infantry
Bady, J., Sergeant, Company A, 93rd, Ohio Infantry
Sharits, Z., Private, Company E, 93rd Ohio Infantry
Young, G.H.., Private, Company A, 95th Ohio Infantry
Reed, Oliver, Private, Company A, 95th Ohio Infantry
McMillan, D.E., Private, Company B, 95th Ohio Infantry
McMillan, D.M., Private, Company B, 95th Ohio Infantry
Miller, P., Private, Company E, 95th Ohio Infantry
Owen, W., Private, Company E, 95th Ohio Infantry

Poycell, H.W., Private, Company E, 95th Ohio Infantry
Poycell, W.W., Private, Company E, 95th Ohio Infantry
Rollins, G.H., Private, Company E, 95th Ohio Infantry
Shaul, W.R., Private, Company E, 95th Ohio Infantry
Little, J.W., Sergeant, Company F, 95th Ohio Infantry
Vanhorn, B., Private, Company F, 95th Ohio Infantry
Jackson, T., Corporal, Company G, 95th Ohio Infantry
Parker, J.A., Private, Company G, 95th Ohio Infantry
Lease, J.W., Corporal, Company I, 95th Ohio Infantry
Wilcox, M., Private, Company I, 95th Ohio Infantry
Wilson, R., Private, Company I, 95th Ohio Infantry
Rush, J., Private, Company L, 95th Ohio Infantry
Hammel, Sam., Private, Company H, 95th Ohio Infantry
McLeary, L., Private, Company B, 96th Ohio Infantry
Poland, J.L., Sergeant, Company B, 97th Ohio Infantry
Cishard, T.R., Private, Company B, 97th Ohio Infantry
Johnson, S., Private, Company B, 97th Ohio Infantry
Stevens, W., Private, Company C, 97th Ohio Infantry
Wilner, R., Private, Company C, 97th Ohio Infantry
Hess, Alexander, Private, Company D, 97th Ohio Infantry
Watts, T.W., Private, Company E, 97th Ohio Infantry
Larkin, W.H., 2nd Lieutenant, Co. H, 97th Ohio Infantry
Emerson, J.G., Private, Company I, 97th Ohio Infantry
Cornwell, J., Sergeant, Company A, 100th Ohio Infantry
McCrory, L.W., Private, Company A, 100th Ohio Infantry
Flemming, J.A., Corporal, Company D, 100th Ohio Infantry
King, A.W., Corporal, Company D, 100th Ohio Infantry
Davis, J., Private, Company D, 100th Ohio Infantry
Hill, G., Private, Company D, 100th Ohio Infantry
Lambert, V., Private, Company D, 100th Ohio Infantry
Wheeler, W., Private, Company D, 100th Ohio Infantry
Sterknell, E.B., Private, Company E, 100th Ohio Infantry
Hiller, R., Sergeant, Company F, 100th Ohio Infantry
Wagner, J., Corporal, Company G, 100th Ohio Infantry
Flegel, John, Corporal, Company K, 100th Ohio Infantry

Dunume, J., Private, Company K, 100th Ohio Infantry
Hofinal, A., Private, Company K, 100th Ohio Infantry
Squire, E.J., 1st Lieutenant, Company D, 101st Ohio Infantry
Rohder, Jacob, Private, Company H, 101st Ohio Infantry
Faggott, Private, Company L, 101st Ohio Infantry
Dilling, A., Private, Company K, 101st Ohio Infantry
Shaffer, J., Private, Company F, 101st Ohio Infantry
Wade, B.F., Sergeant, Company A, 102nd Ohio Infantry
Beanten, J., Private, Company A, 102nd Ohio Infantry
Crawford, E., Private, Company A, 102nd Ohio Infantry
Fabra, D., Private, Company A, 102nd Ohio Infantry
Gein, J., Private, Company A, 102nd Ohio Infantry
McGinness, L., Private, Company A, 102nd Ohio Infantry
Grand, J. Watt, Private, Company A, 102nd Ohio Infantry
Haley, John, Private, Company A, 102nd Ohio Infantry
Hall, L.G., Private, Company A, 102nd Ohio Infantry
Hass, Geo., Private, Company A, 102nd Ohio Infantry
Homer, Jacob, Private, Company A, 102nd Ohio Infantry
Henderson, W., Private, Company A, 102nd Ohio Infantry
Lee, W., Private, Company A, 102nd Ohio Infantry
Merchand, L., Private, Company A, 102nd Ohio Infantry
Mitchell, Jas., Private, Company A, 102nd Ohio Infantry
Peckham, C.R., Private, Company A, 102nd Ohio Infantry
Rose, J.S., Private, Company A, 102nd Ohio Infantry
Ross, Wm., Private, Company A, 102nd Ohio Infantry
Shrader, John, Private, Company A, 102nd Ohio Infantry
Stagle, E.K., Private, Company A, 102nd Ohio Infantry
Stephens, S.S., Private, Company A, 102nd Infantry
Wallace, W.A., Private, Company A, 102nd Ohio Infantry
Richard, R., Private, Company A, 102nd Ohio Infantry
Krebs, H., Corporal, Company B, 102nd Ohio Infantry
Bahn, A., Private, Company B, 102nd Ohio Infantry
McCrea, Private, Company B, 102nd Ohio Infantry
Fisher, D., Private, Company B, 102nd Ohio Infantry
Mercer, J.M., Private, Company B, 102nd Ohio Infantry

Potter, S.R., Private, Company B, 102nd Ohio Infantry
Spafford, H., Private, Company B, 102nd Ohio Infantry
Stocker, S., Private, Company B, 102nd Ohio Infantry
Webster, A., Private, Company B, 102nd Ohio Infantry
Wells, Jos., Private, Company B, 102nd Ohio Infantry
Whissemore, A., Private, Company B, 102nd Ohio Infantry
Woods, M., Private, Company B, 102nd Ohio Infantry
Heimberger, W.C., Sergeant, Company C, 102nd Ohio Infantry
Woltin, P.L., Sergeant, Company C, 102nd Ohio Infantry
Bierly, J., Corporal, Company C, 102nd Ohio Infantry
Beal, Amos, Private, 102nd Ohio Infantry
Flint, B., Private, Company C, 102nd Ohio Infantry
Oyster, Simon, Private, Company C, 102nd Ohio Infantry
Simon, J., Private, Company C, 102nd Ohio Infantry
Wheeler, D., Private, Company C, 102nd Ohio Infantry
Wisler, W., Private, Company C, 102nd Ohio Infantry
Willis, W.W., Private, Company C, 102nd Ohio Infantry
Hosts, J.R., Sergeant, Company D, 102nd Ohio Infantry
Omeveg, G.H., Sergeant, Company D, 102nd Ohio Infantry
Baker, John, Private, Company D, 102nd Ohio Infantry
Bringman, J.D., Private, Company D, 102nd Ohio Infantry
Burt, J.H., Private, Company D, 102nd Ohio Infantry
Errick, W., Private, Company D, 102nd Ohioo Infantry
Grice, David, Private, Company D, 102nd Ohio Infantry
Horn, P.L., Private, Company D, 102nd Ohio Infantry
Keley, J. Mc., Private, Company D, 102nd Ohio Infantry
Kochendewffer, J.H., Private, Company D, 102nd Ohio Infantry
Sidle, H., Private, Company D, 102nd Ohio Infantry
Smutz, G., Private, Company D, 102nd Ohio Infantry
Strawbaugh, S., Private, Company D, 102nd Ohio Infantry
Ulick, G.W., Private, Company D, 102nd Ohio Infantry
Underwood, Jas., Private, Company D, 102nd Ohio Infantry
Warmly, M., Private, Company D, 102nd Ohio Infantry
Williams, J.T., Private, Company D, 102nd Ohio Infantry
Drocliss, J., Corporal, Company E, 102nd Ohio Infantry

Irons, Jacob, Corporal, Company E, 102nd Ohio Infantry
Couter, E., Private, Company E, 102nd Ohio Infantry
Garber, D., Private, Company E, 102nd Ohio Infantry
Lockhart, W., Private, Company E, 102nd Ohio Infantry
Stuff, Fred, Private, Company E, 102nd Ohio Infantry
Anderson, G., Private, Company F, 102nd Ohio Infantry
Keeler, Wm., Private, Company F, 102nd Ohio Infantry
Saunders, J., Private, Company F, 102nd Ohio Infantry
Shepperly, G., Private, Company F, 102nd Ohio Infantry
Shoup, G.W., Private, Company F, 102nd Ohio Infantry
Stine, D.G., Private, Company F, 102nd Ohio Infantry
Torbet, R., Private, Company F, 102nd Ohio Infantry
Hites, Dan, Sergeant, Company G, 102nd Ohio Infantry
Johns, D.W., Corporal, Company G, 102nd Ohio Infantry
Price, S.P., Private, Company G, 102nd Ohio Infantry
Huntsberger, J., Corporal, Company H, 102nd Ohio Infantry
Ball, H., Private, Company H, 102nd Ohio Infantry
Baney, John, Private, Company H, 102nd Ohio Infantry
Bardon, Otto, Private, Company H, 102nd Ohio Infantry
Brenizer, A., Private, Company H, 102nd Ohio Infantry
Brenizer, D., Private, Company H, 102nd Ohio Infantry
Christine, H., Private, Company H, 102nd Ohio Infantry
Crowe, Wm., Private, Company H, 102nd Ohio Infantry
Harrington, G., Private, Company H, 102nd Ohio Infantry
Smith, C., Private, Company H, 102nd Ohio Infantry
Tracy, W.L., Private, Company H, 102nd Ohio Infantry
Wells, Miles, Private, Company H, 102nd Ohio Infantry
Wynn, W.J., Private, Company H, 102nd Ohio Infantry
Fast, W.N., Sergeant, Company K, 102nd Ohio Infantry
Sprinkle, M.H., Sergeant, Company K, 102nd Ohio Infantry
Fast, W.A., Corporal, Company K, 102nd Ohio Infantry
Burnside, R., Private, Company K, 102nd Ohio Infantry
Castle, Jas. L., Private, Company K, 102nd Ohio Infantry
Hartman, J.F., Private, Company K, 102nd Ohio Infantry
Leidig, R., Private, Company K, 102nd Ohio Infantry

Ogden, C.P., Private, Company K, 102nd Ohio Infantry
Singer, J.J., Private, Company K, 102nd Ohio Infantry
Steinmetz, Private, Company K, 102nd Ohio Infantry
Depmer, A., Private, Company A, 103rd Ohio Infantry
Shaw, D., Private, Company D, 103rd Ohio Infantry
Jenet, J., Private, Company H, 103rd Ohio Infantry
Smith, W.W., Private, Company B, 104th Ohio Infantry
Patterson, S., Private, Company F, 104th Ohio Infantry
Winkleman, Private, Company H, 104th Ohio Infantry
Hallet, G,W., Private, Company I, 104th Ohio Infantry
Molton, D., Private, Company I, 104th Ohio Infantry
Smith, B.F., Private, Company A, 105th Ohio Infantry
Joseph, M., Private, Company E, 111th Ohio Infantry
McCord, G.B., 1st Lieutenant, Company F, 111th Ohio Infantry
Hunbarger, S., Private, Company H, 111th Ohio Infantry
Swarm, John L., Private, Company K, 111th Ohio Infantry
Long, B., Private, Company C, 114th Ohio Infantry
Hake, S.T., Captain, Company B, 115th Ohio Infantry
Eadie, John, 1st Lieutenant, Company C, 115th Ohio Infantry
Boosley, Sergeant, Company C, 115th Ohio Infantry
Elay, Jno., Sergeant, Company C, 115th Ohio Infantry
Jones, Arthur, Sergeant, Company C, 115th Ohio Infantry
Way, Chas., W., Sergeant, Company C, 115th Ohio Infantry
Deitrich, C.W., Corporal, Company C, 115th Ohio Infantry
Eadie, J.W., Corporal, Company C, 115th Ohio Infantry
Eatinger, G.W., Corporal, Company C, 115th Ohio Infantry
Everhart, Corporal, Company C, 115th Ohio0 Infantry
Stevens, C., Corporal, Company C, 115th Ohio Infantry
Richardson, H., Corporal, Company C, 115th Ohio Infantry
Tyson, Chas., Corporal, Company C, 115th Ohio Infantry
Garrett, E.W., Musician, Company C, 115th Ohio Infantry
Blair, M.V.B., Private, Company C, 115th Ohio Infantry
Cochran, H., Private, Company C, 115th Ohio Infantry
Cook, J.C., Private, Company C, 115th Ohio Infantry
Cook, J.S., Private, Company C, 115th Ohio Infantry

Coady, Private, Company C, 115th Ohio Infantry
Cross, Geo., Private, Company C, 115th Ohio Infantry
Dickerson, R., Private, Company C, 115th Ohio Infantry
Dolan, James, Private, Company C, 115th Ohio Infantry
Dusonberry, Private, Company C, 115th Ohio Infantry
Doty, Nathan, Private, Company C, 115th Ohio Infantry
Ellers, Edward, Private, Company C, 115th Ohio Infantry
Garrison, J.J., Private, Company C, 115th Ohio Infantry
Greenover, J., Private, Company C, 115th Ohio Infantry
Gulord, Rob't, Private, Company C, 115th Ohio Infantry
Harris, G., Private, Company C, 115th Ohio Infantry
Harris, Jno., Private, Company C, 115th Ohio Infantry
Hume, F.L., Private, Company C, 115th Ohio Infantry
Hurbert, Chas., Private, Company C, 115th Ohio Infantry
King, Edward, Private, Company C, 115th Ohio Infantry
Maley, V.A., Private, Company C, 115th Ohio Infantry
Norton, W.H., Private, Company C, 115th Ohio Infantry
Post, C., Private, Company C, 115th Ohio Infantry
Price, W.D., Private, Company C, 115th Ohio Infantry
Smothers, W., Private, Company C, 115th Ohio Infantry
Stevens, W., Private, Company C, 115th Ohio Infantry
Stout, Chas., Private, Company C, 115th Ohio Infantry
Sysor, Jno., Private, Company C, 115th Ohio Infantry
Weaver, P.A., Private, Company C, 115th Ohio Infantry
Whitmore, Chas., Private, Company C, 115th Ohio Infantry
Whitmore, L., Private, Company C, 115th Ohio Infantry
Woods, Isaac, Private, Company C, 115th Ohio Infantry
Zimmerman, Private, Company C, 115th Ohio Infantry
Hendrick, A.M., Private, Company D, 115th Ohio Infantry
Laffater, A., Private, Company D, 115th Ohio Infantry
Shaffer, J.K., 2nd Lieutenant, Company F, 115th Ohio Infantry
Rue, F., Sergeant, Company F, 115th Ohio Infantry
Smith, W.H.,, Sergeant, Company F, 115th Ohio Infantry
Clapsaddle, F.A., Private, Company F, 115th Ohio Infantry
Crul, B., Private, Company F, 115th Ohio Infantry

James T.H., Private, Company F, 115th Ohio Infantry
Roath, R. W., Private, Company F, 115th Ohio Infantry
Spencer, F., Private, Company F, 115th Ohio Infantry
Thomas, L.A., Private, Company F, 115th Ohio Infantry
Togle, J., Private, Company F, 115th Ohio Infantry
Thompson, E., Sergeant, Company G, 115th Ohio Infantry
Alexander, P.H., Corporal, Company G, 115th Ohio Infantry
Patterson, Jas., Corporal, Company G, 115th Ohio Infantry
Callon, J.C., Private, Company G, 115th Ohio Infantry
Cox, Robt., Private, Company G, 115th Ohio Infantry
Dana, W., Private, Company G, 115th Ohio Infantry
Daro, J.M., Private, Company G, 115th Ohio Infantry
Davis, Wm., Private, Company G, 115th Ohio Infantry
Evans, Thos., Private, Company G, 115th Ohio Infantry
Knapps, C., Private, Company G, 115th Ohio Infantry
Myers, D., Private, Company G, 115th Ohio Infantry
Keney, O., Private, Company F, 116th Ohio Infantry
Robinson, J., Private, Company A, 121st Ohio Infantry
Wallace, H.B., Private, Company A, 124th Ohio Infantry
McDaniel, G., Private, Company D, 124th Ohio Infantry
Adams, Jno., Private, Company A, 125th Ohio Infantry
Watters, S.M., Private, Company H, 125th Ohio Infantry
Lugenbeal, D.W., Private, Company F, 135th Ohio Infantry
Fest, J., Private, Company C, 153rd Ohio Infantry
Van Emore, M.T., Private, Company C, 175th Ohio Infantry
Hendricks, G.W., Private, Company C, 175th Ohio Infantry
Myers, W., Private, Company D, 175th Ohio Infantry
Payne, Jas., Private, Company D, 175th Ohio Infantry
Carroll, W., Private, Company E, 175th Ohio Infantry
Gray, T.J., Private, Company E, 175th Ohio Infantry
Huason, Private, Company G, 175th Ohio Infantry
Morris, Stacy, Private, Company G, 175th Ohio Infantry
Kenard, A., Private, Company C, 183rd Ohio Infantry
Koland, P., Private Company C, 183rd Ohio Infantry
Sugder, A., Private, Company C, 183rd Ohio Infantry

Miller, Jos., Sergeant, Company D, 183rd Ohio Infantry
Polar, G.W., Corporal, Company E, 183rd Ohio Infantry
Gillisman, J., Private, Company F, 183rd Ohio Infantry
Manie, Davis, Private, Company G, 183rd Ohio Infantry
Zephrisharg, Gustave, Sergeant, Co. H, 183rd Ohio Infantry
Barner, Jno., Private, Company H, 183rd Ohio Infantry
Bumgardner, W.J., Company K, 183rd Ohio Infantry
Oliver, Thos., Private, Company K, 183rd Ohio Infantry
Genthar, J., Musician, Company E, 183rd Ohio Infantry
Wade, W.H., Corporal, Company K, 1st Ohio Cavalry
Graham, G., Private, Company A, 2nd Ohio Cavalry
Allman, J., Private, Company A, 2nd Ohio Cavalry
Peas, Jas., Corporal, Company B, 2nd Ohio Cavalry
Russell, C.G., Private, Company G, 2nd Ohio Cavalry
Brown, A.C., Private, Company I, 2nd Ohio Cavalry
Brunner, D., Private, Company K 2nd Ohio Cavalry
Haley, C.C., Private, Company K, 2nd Ohio Cavalry
Donald, H., Private, Company K, 3rd Ohio Cavalry
Erwin, J., Private, Company K, 3rd Ohio Cavalry
Gutton, W.N., Private, Company K, 3rd Ohio Cavalry
Jessow, R., Private, Company K, 3rd Ohio Cavalry
Pickens, L., Private, Company K, 3rd Ohio Cavalry
Pouch, E., Private, Company K, 3rd Ohio Cavalry
Rome, F., Private, Company K, 3rd Ohio Cavalry
Tidwell, C.B., Private, Company K, 3rd Ohio Cavalry
Torvell, H., Private, Company K, 3rd Ohio Cavalry
Wagoner, J., Private, Company K, 3rd Ohio Cavalry
Whiscar, Private, Company K, 3rd Ohio Cavalry
Green, C., Private, Company L, 3rd Ohio Cavalry
Lewis, D.C., 1st Lieutenant, Company M, 3rd Ohio Cavalry
Kertstellar, D., Private, Company M, 3rd Ohio Cavalry
McWethy, C.H., Private, Company M, 3rd Ohio Cavalry
Stoner, J.W., Corporal, McLaughlin's Squadron
Horter, J., Corporal, McLaughlin's Squadron
Noland, Jos., Private, Company H, 4th Ohio Cavalry

Smith, W.H., Sergeant, Company K, 4th Ohio Cavalry
Browne, B., Private, Company L, 4th Ohio Cavalry
Bonkey, N., Sergeant, Company L, 5th Ohio Cavalry
Donnelly, M., Private, Company K, 5th Ohio Cavalry
McMann, M., Private, Company I, 6th Ohio Cavalry
Hanam, T., Sergeant, Company A, 7th Ohio Cavalry
Lascur, A.J., Sergeant, Company A, 7th Ohio Cavalry
Baldwin, J.R., Corporal, Company A, 7th Ohio Cavalry
Gilfiss, W.F., Corporal, Company A, 7th Ohio Cavalry
McCluchy, Corporal, Company A, 7th Ohio Cavalry
Baker, Wm., Private, Company A, 7th Ohio Cavalry
Bell, J.K., Private, Company A, 7th Ohio Cavalry
Botts, Thos., Private, Company A, 7th Ohio Cavalry
Brickett, Private, Company A, 7th Ohio Cavalry
Burbink, A., Private, Company A, 7th Ohio Cavalry
Cameron, B., Private, Company A, 7th Ohio Cavalry
Daona, J., Private, Company A, 7th Ohio Cavalry
Dugan, W., Private, Company A, 7th Ohio Cavalry
Drum, Chas., Private, Company A, 7th Ohio Cavalry
Fanning, A., Private, Company A, 7th Ohio Cavalry
Faulkner, J., Private, Company A, 7th Ohio Cavalry
Folz, P., Private, Company A, 7th Ohio Cavalry
Hill, G., Private, Company A, 7th Ohio Cavalry
Hoyt, J., Private, Company A, 7th Ohio Cavalry
McChollister, C., Private, Company A, 7th Ohio Cavalry
McDaniel, J., Private, Company A, 7th Ohio Cavalry
Morganthater, J., Private, Company A, 7th Ohio Cavalry
Orbey, F., Private, Company A, 7th Ohio Cavalry
Robb, R.D., Private, Company A, 7th Ohio Cavalry
Shannard, T.W., Private, Company A, 7th Ohio Cavalry
Shecrick, S.A., Private, Company A, 7th Ohio Cavalry
Trenol, I., Private, Company A, 7th Ohio Cavalry
Woodward, T., Private, Company A, 7th Ohio Cavalry
Harr, R., Private, Company B, 7th Ohio Cavalry
Harrison, L.D., Private, Company B, 7th Ohio Cavalry

Maxwell, J.J., Private, Company B, 7th Ohio Cavalry
Lenyshaw, C., Private, Company D, 7th Ohio Cavalry
Dickson, A.C., Private, Company E, 7th Ohio Cavalry
Rieble, W., Private, Company E, 7th Ohio Cavalry
Weights, A.W., Private, Company E, 7th Ohio Cavalry
Starrett, J.H., Private, Company F, 7th Ohio Cavalry
Curley, J.J., Private, Company F, 7th Ohio Cavalry
Sharp, J., Private, Company G, 7th Ohio Cavalry
Laffin, J., Hos Steward, ...Cavalry
Shultz, E., Private, Company A, 9th Ohio Cavalry
Gram, W., Private, Company C, 9th Ohio Cavalry
Davis, M.J., Sergeant, Company D, 9th Ohio Cavalry
Jopp, Jos., Corporal, Company D, 9th Ohio Cavalry
Hanson, Thos., Private, Company E, 9th Ohio Cavalry
Certcher, J., Private, Company F, 9th Ohio Cavalry
Molten, W.P., Private, Company F, 9th Ohio Cavalry
Mankin, T., Private, Company H, 9th Ohio Cavalry
Heager, G., Sergeant, Company F, 9th Ohio Cavalry
Brown, I., Private, Company K, 9th Ohio Cavalry
Kirker, W., Private, Company K, 9th Ohio Cavalry
Wright, F., Private, Company M, 9th Ohio Cavalry
Taylor, C., Private, Company A, 10th Ohio Cavalry
Bader, P.H., Sergeant, Company B, 10th Ohio Cavalry
Jennings, J., Private, Company B, 10th Ohio Cavalry
Morgan, John, Private, Company B, 19th Ohio Cavalry
Taylor, A., Private, Company G, 10th Ohio Cavalry
Burnett, J., Private, Company M, 10th Ohio Cavalry
Hunter, A.E., Private, Company M, 10th Ohio Cavalry
Hayner, E., Private, Company A, 12th Ohio Cavalry
Roberts, C., Private, Company E, 12th Ohio Cavalry
Roberts, C.A., Private, Company E, 12th Ohio Cavalry
Collins, P., Corporal, Company K, 12th Ohio Cavalry
Clancey, W.F., Hos Steward, 20th Ohio Cavalry
Long, G.M., Corporal, Company E, 20th Ohio Cavalry
Lawstead, H.P., Private, Company E, 20th Ohio Cavalry

Bothenbaugh, E., Private, Company K, 20th Ohio Cavalry
Coup, D., Private, Company D, 28th Ohio Cavalry
Rinehart, J., Sergeant, 22nd Ohio Battery
Kerns, L., Private, Company C, 1st Tennessee Cavalry
Powell, John, Private, Company A, 2nd Tennessee Cavalry
King, Geo., Private, Company B, 2nd Tennessee Cavalry
Atchley, T., Private, Company C, 2nd Tennessee Cavalry
Meek, R., Private, Company C, 2nd Tennessee Cavalry
Jack, M., Private, Company F, 2nd Tennessee Cavalry
Knight, J., Private, Company F, 2nd Tennessee Cavalry
Culp, A.J., Private, Company G, 2nd Tennessee Cavalry
Lost, D.M., Private, Company G, 2nd Tennessee Cavalry
Patton, R.E., Private, Company K, 3rd Tennessee Cavalry
Pillington, A., Private, Company K, 3rd Tennessee Cavalry
Cowan, S.A., Sergeant, Company A, 3rd Tennessee Cavalry
Franelin, J.R., Sergeant, Company A, 3rd Tennessee Cavalry
Rule, A.M., Sergeant, Company A, 3rd Tennessee Cavalry
Bell, F.M., Corporal, Company A, 3rd Tennessee Cavalry
Donnellson, D.D., Corporal, Co. A, 3rd Tennessee Cavalry
Kidd, Alexander, Corporal, Company A, 3rd Tennessee Cavalry
Rodgers, M.H., Corporal, Company A, 3rd Tennessee Cavalry
Copeland, J., Private, Company A, 3rd Tennessee Cavalry
Curtiss, J.T., Private, Company A, 3rd Tennessee Cavalry
Dunlape, S.P., Private, Company A, 3rd Tennessee Cavalry
Everett, Jas., Private, Company A, 3rd Tennessee Cavalry
Farmer, A., Private, Company A, 3rd Tennessee Cavalry
Farmer, E., Private, Company A, 3rd Tennessee Cavalry
Farmer, J., Private, Company A, 3rd Tennessee Cavalry
Finley, B.M., Private, Company A, 3rd Tennessee Cavalry
Gamble, M., Private, Company A, 3rd Tennessee Cavalry
Hasser, A., Private, Company A, 3rd Tennessee Cavalry
Hasser, H., Private, Company A, 3rd Tennessee Cavalry
Hausser, L., Private, Company A, 3rd Tennessee Cavalry
Hedrick, D., Private, Company A, 3rd Tennessee Cavalry
Jeffers, Wm., Private, Company A, 3rd Tennessee Cavalry

Keeble, J.H., Private, Company A, 3rd Tennessee Cavalry
Kemble, J.H., Private, Company A, 3rd Tennessee Cavalry
Kidd, J.W., Private, Company A, 3rd Tennessee Cavalry
Kidd, L.M., Private, Company A, 3rd Tennessee Cavalry
Osulivan, R.T., Private, Company A, 3rd Tennessee Cavalry
Patty, J.A., Private, Company A, 3rd Tennessee Cavalry
Payne, J.P., Private, Company A, 3rd Tennessee Cavalry
Phelps, John, Private, Company A, 3rd Tennessee Cavalry
Phelps, Wm., Private, Company A, 3rd Tennessee Cavalry
Pulmons, T.J., Private, Company A, 3rd Tennessee Cavalry
Rale, B., Private, Company A, 3rd Tennessee Cavalry
Russen, B., Private, Company A, 3rd Tennessee Cavalry
Russell, N., Private, Company A, 3rd Tennessee Cavalry
Splann, A., Private, Company A, 3rd Tennessee Cavalry
Thompson, U., Private, Company A, 3rd Tennessee Cavalry
Tipton, C., Private, Company A, 3rd Tennessee Cavalry
Wilson, A., Private, Company A, 3rd Tennessee Cavalry
Vineyard, W.T., Private, Company A, 3rd Tennessee Cavalry
Carver, Wm., Sergeant, Company B, 3rd Tennessee Cavalry
Conellson, J.B., Sergeant, Company B, 3rd Tennessee Cavalry
Davis, G.C., Sergeant, Company B, 3rd Tennessee Cavalry
Davis, J.A., Sergeant, Company B, 3rdTennessee Cavalry
Tipton, A., Sergeant, Company B, 3rdTennessee Cavalry
Leise, Adam, Corporal, Company B, 3rd Tennessee Cavalry
McClanihan, D., Corporal, Company B, 3rd Tennessee Cavalry
Millsap, J., Corporal, Company B, 3rd Tennessee Cavalry
Bailey, W., Private, Company B, 3rd Tennessee Cavalry
Brown, M.S., Private, Company B, 3rd Tennessee Cavalry
Brown, T.M., Private, Company B, 3rd Tennessee Cavalry
Byron, J.H., Private, Company B, 3rd Tennessee Cavalry
Carver, J., Private, Company B, 3rd Tennessee Cavalry
Ellenberry, J., Private, Company B, 3rd Tennessee Cavalry
Finger, A., Private, Company B, 3rd Tennessee Cavalry
Hand, John F., Private, Company B, Tennessee Cavalry
Lackly, J.B., Private, Company B, 3rd Tennessee Cavalry

Leak, Jas., Private, Company B, 3rd Tennessee Cavalry
Milsap, W., Private, Company B, 3rd Tennessee Cavalry
Pinkney, W.C., Private, Company B, 3rd Tennessee Cavalry
Prayer, Jos., Private, Company B, 3rd Tennessee Cavalry
Purger, Wm., Private, Company B, 3rd Tennessee Cavalry
Rodger, T.W., Private, Company B, 3rd Tennessee Cavalry
Rolen, B.W., Private, Company B, 3rd Tennessee Cavalry
Swaggerty, Wm. S., Private, Co. B, 3rd Tennessee Cavalry
Tipton, Jas., Private, Company B, 3rd Tennessee Cavalry
Cortney, J.S., Sergeant, Company C, 3rd Tennessee Cavalry
Dyer, S.A., Sergeant, Company C, 3rd Tennessee Cavalry
Mattock, G., Sergeant, Company C, 3rd Tennessee Cavalry
Wade, W.D., Sergeant, Company C, 3rd Tennessee Cavalry
Brown, P.H., Corporal, Company C, 3rd Tennessee Cavalry
Cortney, W.S., Corporal, Company C, 3rd Tennessee Cavalry
Cox, Jesse, Corporal, Company C, 3rd Tennessee Cavalry
Lutrell, W., Corporal, Company C, 3rd Tennessee Cavalry
McPhail, D.M., Corporal, Company C, 3rd Tennessee Cavalry
Shortz, J.W., Corporal, Company C, 3rd Tennessee Cavalry
Varnell, A.P., Corporal, Company C, 3rd Tennessee Cavalry
Wade, J.W., Corporal, Company C, 3rd Tennessee Cavalry
Bishop, John, Private, Company C, 3rd Tennessee Cavalry
Bishop, W., Private, Company C, 3rd Tennessee Cavalry
Brandon, Jno. Private, Company C, 3rd Tennessee Cavalry
Dickerson, J., Private, Company C, 3rd Tennessee Cavalry
Golden, J., Private, Company C, 3^{ld} Tennessee Cavalry
Graham, L., Private, Company C, 3rd Tennessee Cavalry
Hickman, B., Private, Company C, 3rd Tennessee Cavalry
Hoback, G., Private, Company C, 3rd Tennessee Cavalry
Kennedy, G.W., Private, Company C, 3rd Tennessee Cavalry
Kinsha, G.S., Private, Company C, 3rd Tennessee Cavalry
Mann, W.S., Private, Company C, 3rd Tennessee Cavalry
McPhail, B., Private, Company C, 3rd Tennessee Cavalry
Mills, J.F., Private, Company C, 3rd Tennessee Cavalry
Myers, J., Private, Company C, 3rd Tennessee Cavalry

Neilor, W.N., Private, Company C, 3rd Tennessee Cavalry
Newman, G., Private, Company C, 3rd Tennessee Cavalry
Palmer, W.N., Private, Company C, 3rd Tennessee Cavalry
Rease, L., Private, Company C, 3rd Tennessee Cavalry
Richter, H., Private, Company C, 3rd Tennessee Cavalry
Riddle, J.R., Private, Company C, 3rd Tennessee Cavalry
Robinson, Jas., Private, Company C, 3rd Tennessee Cavalry
Ronimes, L., Private, Company C, 3rd Tennessee Cavalry
Russell, O., Private, Company C, 3rd Tennessee Cavalry
Scott, Jas., Private, Company C, 3rd Tennessee Cavalry
Stroud, J.N., Private, Company C, 3rd Tennessee Cavalry
Trobaugh, I., Private, Company C, 3rd Tennessee Cavalry
Wood, J.E., Private, Company C, 3rd Tennessee Cavalry
Wood, L., Private, Company C, 3rd Tennessee Cavalry
Wood, Jno., Private, Company C, 3rd Tennessee Cavalry
Harin, W., Sergeant, Company D, 3rd Tennessee Cavalry
Hines, O.E., Sergeant, Company D, 3rd Tennessee Cavalry
Hooper, J.H., Sergeant, Company D, 3rd Tennessee Cavalry
Mansfield, W.S., Sergeant, Company D, 3rd Tennessee Cavalry
Maxwell, G. W., Sergeant, Company D, 3rd Tennessee Cavalry
Douglass, J.E., Corporal, Company D, 3rd Tennessee Cavalry
Elsey, R.M., Corporal, Company D, 3rd Tennessee Cavalry
Harris, Wm., Corporal, Company D, 3rd Tennessee Cavalry
Nichols D., Corporal, Company D, 3rd Tennessee Cavalry
Strickley, M., Corporal, Company D, 3rd Tennessee Cavalry
Wadell, S.M., Corporal, Company D, 3rd Tennessee Cavalry
Demman, T., Private, Company D, 3rd Tennessee Cavalry
Fergeson, J.H., Private, Company D, 3rd Tennessee Cavalry
Haffager, J.W., Private, Company D, 3rd Tennessee Cavalry
Henry, J.W., Private, Company D, 3rd Tennessee Cavalry
Long, A., Private, Company D, 3rd Tennessee Cavalry
Long, John, Private, Company D, 3rd Tennessee Cavalry
Pierce, R.M., Private, Company D, 3rd Tennessee Cavalry
Saylor, John, Private, Company D, 3rd Tennessee Cavalry
Smith, W.D., Private, Company D, 3rd Tennessee Cavalry

Kidd, James, Sergeant, Company E, 3rd Tennessee Cavalry
Landers, D., Sergeant, Company E, 3rd Tennessee Cavalry
Rice, John, Sergeant, Company E, 3rd Tennessee Cavalry
Anderson, Jas., Corporal, Company E, 3rd Tennessee Cavalry
Griffin, H., Corporal, Company E, 3rd Tennessee Cavalry
Johnson, J. M., Corporal, Company E 3rd Tennessee Cavalry
Meinsel, Corporal, Company E, 3rd Tennessee Cavalry
Miller, J.W., Corporal, Company E, 3rd Tennessee Cavalry
Swaggerty, S., Corporal, Company E, 3rd Tennessee Cavalry
Way, M.V., Corporal, Company E, 3rd Tennessee Cavalry
Whittenberger, D.A., Corporal, Co. E, 3rd Tennessee Cavalry
Williams, S.H., Corporal, Company E, 3rd Tennessee Cavalry
Baker, W.A., Corporal, Company E, 3rd Tennessee Cavalry
Basley, W.J., Corporal, Company E, 3rd Tennessee Cavalry
Bennett, E.M., Corporal, Company E, 3rd Tennessee Cavalry
Burnette, O.H., Corporal, Company E, 3rd Tennessee Cavalry
Crusoe, Wm. R., Corporal, Company E, 3rd Tennessee Cavalry
Hamilton, R.N., Corporal, Company E, 3rd Tennessee Cavalry
Henderson, J.C., Corporal, Company E, 3rd Tennessee Cavalry
Hicks, J.H., Corporal, Company E, 3rd Tennessee Cavalry
Hines, Joseph, Corporal, Company E, Tennessee Cavalry
Murphy, E.A., Corporal, Company E, Tennessee Cavalry
Murphy, J.M., Corporal, Company E, Tennessee Cavalry
Ottinger, M., Corporal, Company E, 3rd Tennessee Cavalry
Simpson, I.H., Corporal, Company E, 3rd Tennessee Cavalry
Thomas, Marion, Corporal, Company E, 3rd Tennessee Cavalry
Allen, J.F., Sergeant, Company F, 3rd Tennessee Cavalry
Bailey, R.M., Sergeant, Company F, 3rd Tennessee Cavalry
Hamilton, H.C., Sergeant, Company F, 3rd Tennessee Cavalry
Lee, E., Sergeant, Company F, 3rd Tennessee Cavalry
Estes, J., Corporal, Company F, 3rd Tennessee Cavalry
Bogert, C.H., Private, Company F, Tennessee Cavalry
Bogert, S.F., Private, Company F, 3rd Tennessee Cavalry
Bookout, J.L., Private, Company F, 3rd Tennessee Cavalry
Cochran, H., Private, Company F, 3rd Tennessee Cavalry

Collins, J.R., Private, Company F, 3rd Tennessee Cavalry
Conner, G.W., Private, Company F, 3rd Tennessee Cavalry
Doherty, J.M., Private, Company F, 3rd Tennessee Cavalry
Elliott, J.W., Private, Company F, 3rd Tennessee Cavalry
Fuller, Jas., Private, Company F, 3rd Tennessee Cavalry
Fugerson, W.H., Private, Company F, Tennessee Cavalry
Howell, E., Private, Company F, 3rd Tennessee Cavalry
Jones, O.C., Private, Company F, 3rd Tennessee Cavalry
Leonard T.J., Private, Company F, 3rd Tennessee Cavalry
Long, M.B., Private, Company F, 3rd Tennessee Cavalry
Marr, B.L., Private, Company F, 3rd Tennessee Cavalry
McClure, M.D., Private, Company F, 3rd Tennessee Cavalry
Milton, Wm., Private, Company F, 3rd Tennessee Cavalry
Mussin, H.W., Private, Company F, 3rd Tennessee Cavalry
Reed, R., Private, Company F, 3rd Tennessee Cavalry
Smith, J.R., Private, Company F, 3rd Tennessee Cavalry
Spongle, G., Private, Company F, 3rd Tennessee Cavalry
Stone, W., Private, Company F, 3rd Tennessee Cavalry
Ursery, J.R., Private, Company F, 3rd Tennessee Cavalry
Whiteman, R., Private, Company F, 3rd Tennessee Cavalry
Williams, N.G., Private, Company F, 3rd Tennessee Cavalry
Beard, J.O., Sergeant, Company G, 3rd Tennessee Cavalry
Turner, R., Sergeant, Company G, 3rd Tennessee Cavalry
Williams, D.M., Corporal, Company G, 3rd Tennessee Cavalry
Williams, Jesse, Corporal, Company G, 3rd Tennessee Cavalry
Baker, G., Private, Company G, 3rd Tennessee Cavalry
Baker, Jacob, Private, Company G, 3rd Tennessee Cavalry
Baker, John, Private, Company G, 3rd Tennessee Cavalry
Brooks, Joseph, Private, Company G, 3rd Tennessee Cavalry
Cantrell, Jno., Private, Company G, 3rd Tennessee Cavalry
Campbell, N.J., Private, Company G, 3rd Tennessee Cavalry
Collins, J.H., Private, Company G, 3rd Tennessee Cavalry
Cunningham, Jas., Company G, 3rd Tennessee Cavalry
Curtin, R.A., Private, Company G, 3rd Tennessee Cavalry
Gross, A., Private, Company G, 3rd Tennessee Cavalry

Hamilton, Jas., Private, Company G, 3rd Tennessee Cavalry
Hudson, P., Private, Company G, 3rd Tennessee Cavalry
Humbrick, Jno., Private, Company G, 3rd Tennessee Cavalry
Johnson, W.R., Private, Company G, 3rd Tennessee Cavalry
Lee, Jas., Private, Company G, 3rd Tennessee Cavalry
McClauson, J.M., Private, Company G, 3rd Tennessee Cavalry
Millard, L.R., Private, Company G, 3rd Tennessee Cavalry
Mills, W., Private, Company G, 3rd Tennessee Cavalry
Padyot, B., Private, Company G, 3rd Tennessee Cavalry
Wylers, L., Private, Company G, 3rd Tennessee Cavalry
Walker, D.B., Private, Company G, 3rd Tennessee Cavalry
Brown, M.E., Sergeant, Company H, 3rd Tennessee Cavalry
Evitt, W., Sergeant, Company H, 3rd Tennessee Cavalry
Jones, J.W., Sergeant, Company H, 3rd Tennessee Cavalry
Barnett, A., Private, Company H, 3rd Tennessee Cavalry
Cursick, D., Private, Company H, 3rd Tennessee Cavalry
Farmer, E., Private, Company H, 3rd Tennessee Cavalry
Farmer, J.O., Private, Company H, 3rd Tennessee Cavalry
Farrer, G., Private, Company H, 3rd Tennessee Cavalry
Firrett, Wm., Private, Company H, 3rd Tennessee Cavalry
Hickox, J.E., Private, Company H, 3rd Tennessee Cavalry
Hessinger, H.P., Private, Company H, 3rd Tennessee Cavalry
Johnson, A., Private, Company H, 3rd Tennessee Cavalry
Lopt, J.H., Private, Company H, 3rd Tennessee Cavalry
Massey, J.J., Private, Company H, 3rd Tennessee Cavalry
DeAmond, H.H., Sergeant, Company I, 3rd Tennessee Cavalry
Fowler, A., Sergeant, Company I, 3rd Tennessee Cavalry
Frazier, J., Sergeant, Company I, 3rd Tennessee Cavalry
Howard, T.A., Sergeant, Company I, 3rd Tennessee Cavalry
Linconfelter, H., Sergeant, Company I, 3rd Tennessee Cavalry
Rhed, P., Sergeant, Company I, 3rd Tennessee Cavalry
Murphy, Jno., Corporal, Company I, 3rd Tennessee Cavalry
Russell, R.T., Corporal, Company I, 3rd Tennessee Cavalry
Atchley, P.A., Private, Company I, 3rd Tennessee Cavalry
Atsher, Wm., Private, Company I, 3rd Tennessee Cavalry

Bagart, M., Private, Company I, 3rd Tennessee Cavalry
Bean, P., Private, Company I, 3rd Tennessee Cavalry
Brock, J.A., Private, Company I, 3rd Tennessee Cavalry
Cooper, Rob't, Private, Company I, 3rd Tennessee Cavalry
Crawford, H.P., Private, Company I, 3rd Tennessee Cavalry
Dailey, John, Private, Company I, 3rd Tennessee Cavalry
Draper, D.S., Private, Company I, 3rd Tennessee Cavalry
Dunlap, A.B., Private, Company I, 3rd Tennessee Cavalry
Ellison, Thos., Private, Company I, 3rd Tennessee Cavalry
Evans, S.M., Private, Company I, 3rd Tennessee Cavalry
Gibson, D., Private, Company I, 3rd Tennessee Cavalry
Hayden, D.A., Private, Company I, 3rd Tennessee Cavalry
Hill, W.S., Private, Company I, 3rd Tennessee Cavalry
Hines, Jas., Private, Company I, 3rd Tennessee Cavalry
Hockney, L., Private, Company I, 3rd Tennessee Cavalry
Johns, W., Private, Company I, 3rd Tennessee Cavalry
Johnson, Jacob, Private, Company I, Tennessee Cavalry
Kaywood, B.F., Private, Company I, 3rd Tennessee Cavalry
Kirkpatrick, J.R., Private, Company I, 3rd Tennessee Cavalry
Kirkpatrick, W.C., Private, Company I, 3rd Tennessee Cavalry
Linconfelter, G.T., Private, Company I, 3rd Tennessee Cavalry
Lindsay, J.R., Private, Company I, 3rd Tennessee Cavalry
McKann, A., Private, Company I, 3rd Tennessee Cavalry
McTeag, D., Private, Company I, 3rd Tennessee Cavalry
Morrison, G.C., Private, Company I, 3rd Tennessee Cavalry
Noe, Wm., Private, Company I, 3rd Tennessee Cavalry
Rodgers, W.J., Private, Company I, 3rd Tennessee Cavalry
Rodgers, J., Private, Company I, 3rd Tennessee Cavalry
Romins, G.R., Private, Company I, 3rd Tennessee Cavalry
Romins, S., Private, Company I, 3rd Tennessee Cavalry
Scott, James, Private, Company I, 3rd Tennessee Cavalry
Simpson, A.A., Private, Company I, 3rd Tennessee Cavalry
Simpson, J.G., Private, Company I, 3rd Tennessee Cavalry
Stanley, M., Private, Company I, 3rd Tennessee Cavalry
Stevens, Jno., Private, Company I, 3rd Tennessee Cavalry

Summey, Jas., Private, Company I, 3rd Tennessee Cavalry
Thompson, R., 1st Sergeant, Co. K, 3rd Tennessee Cavalry
Wayland, L.A., Sergeant, Company K, 3rd Tennessee Cavalry
Caree, Jas. P., Corporal, Company K, 3rd Tennessee Cavalry
Cash, H.W., Corporal, Company K, 3rd Tennessee Cavalry
Rule, I., Corporal, Company K, 3rd Tennessee Cavalry
Allen, David, Private, Company K, 3rd Tennessee Cavalry
Battles, I., Private, Company K, 3rd Tennessee Cavalry
Battles, W.F., Private, Company K, 3rd Tennessee Cavalry
Beggett, J.D., Private, Company K, 3rd Tennessee Cavalry
Blane, M., Private, Company K, 3rd Tennessee Cavalry
Chandler, B., Private, Company K, 3rd Tennessee Cavalry
Davis, E., Private, Company K, 3rd Tennessee Cavalry
Davis, Wm., Private, Company K, 3rd Tennessee Cavalry
Dearman, L., Private, Company K, 3rd Tennessee Cavalry
Dearman, Sol., Private, Company K, 3rd Tennessee Cavalry
Finger, F., Private, Company K, 3rd Tennessee Cavalry
Hodges, J.W., Private Company K, 3rd Tennessee Cavalry
Kinneman, J.M., Private, Company K, 3rd Tennessee Cavalry
Lansom, G.M., Private, Company K, 3rd Tennessee Cavalry
Leak, Wm., Private, Company K, 3rd Tennessee Cavalry
McMurry, R.R., Private, Company K, 3rd Tennessee Cavalry
Ramsey, M., Private, Company K, 3rd Tennessee Cavalry
Reed, Wm. M., Private, Company K, Tennessee Cavalry
Rule, C., Private, Company K, 3rd Tennessee Cavalry
Scroggs, Isaac, Private, Company K, 3rd Tennessee Cavalry
Smith, J.P., Private, Company K, 3rd Tennessee Cavalry
Williams, E., Private, Company K, 3rd Tennessee Cavalry
Knight, J.D., Sergeant, Company L, 3rd Tennessee Cavalry
Mansfield, Z.M., Sergeant, Company L, 3rd Tennessee Cavalry
Hurry, J., Corporal, Company L, 3rd Tennessee Cavalry
Jenkins, S., Corporal, Company L, 3rd Tennessee Cavalry
Lemon, L., Corporal, Company L, 3rd Tennessee Cavalry
Montgomery, J.L, Corporal, Co. L, 3rd Tennessee Cavalry
Wiggins, N.C., Corporal, Company L, 3rd Tennessee Cavalry

Hancock, W.B., Private, Company L, 3rd Tennessee Cavalry
Hinchy, L.C., Private, Company L, 3rd Tennessee Cavalry
Renlan, Thos., Private, Company L, 3rd Tennessee Cavalry
Rodgers, Wm., Private, Company L, 3rd Tennessee Cavalry
Robinson, H., Private, Company M, 3rd Tennessee Cavalry
McDowell, Wm., 1st Lieutenant, Co. A, 4th Tennessee Cavalry
Station, Henry, Sergeant, Company A, 4th Tennessee Cavalry
Dickens, Newton, Private, Company A, 4th Tennessee Cavalry
Dronsgea, R., Private, Company A, 4th Tennessee Cavalry
Hastshan, R., Private, Company A, 4th Tennessee Cavalry
McMurry, W., Private, Company A, 4th Tennessee Cavalry
Odin, P.H., Private, Company A, 4th Tennessee Cavalry
Sumner, J.B., Private, Company A, 4th Tennessee Cavalry
Develin, Jas., Private, Company C, 4th Tennessee Cavalry
Norman, J., Private, Company H, 4th Tennessee Cavalry
Bayless, W., Private, Company I, 4th Tennessee Cavalry
Thomas, H., Private, Company L, 4th Tennessee Cavalry
Phelps, O., Private, Company L, 5th Tennessee Cavalry
Sheton, O.G., Private, Company E, 5th Tennessee Cavalry
Gray, M.L., Private, Company G, 6th Tennessee Cavalry
Walberton, Private, Company G, 6th Tennessee Cavalry
Derryburg, J.H., Private, Company A, 7th Tennessee Cavalry
Smith, J., Private, Company C, 7th Tennessee Cavalry
Harover, John, Private, Company D, 7th Tennessee Cavalry
Small, H.J., Private, Company H, 7th Tennessee Cavalry
Campbell, W., Private, Company K, 7th Tennessee Cavalry
Davenport, J.K., Private, Company K, 7th Tennessee Cavalry
Montgomery, C., Private, Company A, 8th Tennessee Cavalry
Nevins, L., Private, Company A, 8th Tennessee Cavalry
Minsey, R., Private, Company B, 8th Tennessee Cavalry
Husted, T.D., Private, Company C, 11th Tennessee Cavalry
White, James, Corporal, Company D, 11th Tennessee Cavalry
Pierce, R., Private, Company C, 12th Tennessee Cavalry
Brownley, J.B., Private, Company A, 2nd Tennessee Mt'd Inf.
Emenery, W., Private, Company A, 2nd Tennessee Mt'd Inf.

Grier, J.A., Private, Company A, 2nd Tennessee Mt'd Inf.
Moffatt, Jas., Private, Company C, 2nd Tennessee Mt'd Inf.
Rease, W., Sergeant, Company G, 2nd Tennessee Mt'd Inf.
Anderson, J.F., Corporal, Company I, 3rd Tennessee Infantry
Ramsey, M.C., Private, Company I, 3rd Tennessee Infantry
Foster, H.C., Private, Company A, 1st Virginia Cavalry
Manner, A., Private, Company A, 1st Virginia Cavalry
Cruddu, W.A., Private, Company D, 1st Virginia Cavalry
McHenry, Jas., Private, Company D, 1st Virginia Cavalry
Smith, G.G., Private, Company D, 1st Virginia Cavalry
Stephens, A., Private, Company D, 1st Virginia Cavalry
Craig, Anthony, Private, Company C, 1st Virginia Cavalry
Reeble, C., Private, Company G, 1st Virginia Cavalry
Loy, George C., Private, Company I, 1st Virginia Cavalry
Stafford, S.D.L., Private, Company L, 3rd Virginia Cavalry
Woodyard, L., Private, Company A, 4th Virginia Cavalry
Stelle, J.N., Private, Company C, 5th Virginia Cavalry
Lyons, J.H., Corporal, Company B, 6th Virginia Cavalry
Lawless, E., Private, Company B, 6th Virginia Cavalry
Match, John, Private, Company K, 6th Virginia Cavalry
Morris, Jas., Private, Company H, 6th Virginia Cavalry
Talmadge, J., Private, Company H, 6th Virginia Cavalry
Wilson, T.P., Private, Company H, 6th Virginia Cavalry
Hall, J.F., Sergeant, Company I, 6th Virginia Cavalry
Johnson, H., Sergeant, Company I, 6th Virginia Cavalry
Parker, J.R., Corporal, Company I, 6th Virginia Cavalry
Tucker, G.W., Corporal, Company I, 6th Virginia Cavalry
Dabney, G., Private, Company I, 6th Virginia Cavalry
Jones, Stephen, Private, Company I, 6th Virginia Cavalry
Maury, C.R., Private, Company I, 6th Virginia Cavalry
McDaniel, J.W., Private, Company I, 6th Virginia Cavalry
McDowell F.M., Private, Company I, 6th Virginia Cavalry
Oaley, W., Private, Company I, 6th Virginia Cavalry
Rhodes, A., Private, Company I, 6th Virginia Cavalry
McEwen, Jas., Captain, Company K, 6th Virginia Cavalry

Burns, Pat, Private, Company K, 6th Virginia Cavalry
Elder, J.J., Private, Company K, 6th Virginia Cavalry
Hughes, H., Private, Company K, 6th Virginia Cavalry
Martin, J.H., Private, Company K, 6th Virginia Cavalry
McCubber, J.B., Private, Company K, 6th Virginia Cavalry
Bradley, G., Private, Company A, 7th Virginia Cavalry
Goodflasher, G.W., Private, Company A, 7th Virginia Cavalry
Carderlle, W.M., Private, Company C, 7th Virginia Cavalry
Handorf, Jno. H., Private, Company F, 7th Virginia Cavalry
English, W., Private, Company F, 7th Virginia Cavalry
Mass, Jas., Private, Company F, 7th Virginia Cavalry
Ragsdale, Robert, Private, Company F, 7th Virginia Cavalry
Riley, Jno., Private, Company F, 7th Virginia Cavalry
Willhelm, C., Private, Company F, 7th Virginia Cavalry
Mallaby, M., Private, Company G, 7th Virginia Cavalry
Creen, A.W., Sergeant, Company L, 7th Virginia Cavalry
McKnight, J., Private, Company L, 7th Virginia Cavalry
Scott, Thos., Private, Company L, 7th Virginia Cavalry
Roberts, J.R., Private, Company L, 7th Virginia Cavalry
Mattlinger, J., Private, Company L, 7th Virginia Cavalry
Barett, J.T., 2nd Lieutenant, Company A, 12th Virginia Cavalry
Gambol, H., Private, Company B, 14th Virginia Cavalry
Cornell, E., Private, Company G, 14th Virginia Cavalry
Bartlett, E.M., Private, Company C, 16th Virginia Cavalry
Springer, S., Private, Company E, 16th Virginia Cavalry

Persons Known To Have Been On Board
But Not Reported In The Official List

Sanders, S.F., Company I, 137th Illinois
Frazee, Martin, Company C, 2nd Indiana Cavalry
Lee, Asa, Company A, 6th Indiana Cavalry
Kline, Henry J., Company G, 9th Indiana Cavalry
Mayes, J.H., Company C, 40th Indiana Cavalry
Stewart, Geo. W., Company D, 40th Indiana Cavalry
Hazellaige, Captain, Company K, 40th Indiana Cavalry
Taylor, Joe, Lieutenant, 124th Indiana Infantry
May, John, 137th Indiana Cavalry
Williams, 1st Kentucky Cavalry
Gambill, Henry, Company B, 14th Kentucky Infantry
Curnsitte, Elisha, Company G, 14th Kentucky Infantry
Hamlin, O.E., Company E, 2nd Michigan Cavalry
Johnson, B.F., Company A, 5th Michigan Cavalry
Clarkson, Geo. A., Company H, 5th Michigan Cavalry
Norton, Henry, Company B, 8th Michigan Cavalry
White, Manly C., Company B, 8th Michigan Cavalry
Kinney, John, 8th Michigan Cavalry
Wendt, Wm., Company L, 8th Michigan Cavalry
Dunsmore, J.W., Company I, 1st Michigan E and M
Stevens, Joseph, Company E, 4th Michigan Infantry
Hindes, Elias, Company A, 18th Michigan Infantry
Jones, A., Company B, 18th Michigan Infantry
Smith, O.W., Company B, 18th Michigan Infantry
Thayer, C., Company B, 18th Michigan Infantry
Porter, W.G., Company C, 18th Michigan Infantry
Larkey, Pat, Company E, 18th Michigan Infantry
Hohns, M., Company F, 18th Michigan Infantry
Aldrich, H.C., Sergeant, Company G, 18th Michigan Infantry
West, C.A., Company G, 18th Michigan Infantry
Nicholas, C., Company H, 18th Michigan Infantry
Hampton, E., Company I, 18th Michigan Infantry

Upton, H.H., Company I, 18th Michigan Infantry
Hinds, T.J., Company K, 18th Michigan Infantry
Mann, Jas. H., Company K, 18th Michigan Infantry
Metta, A.R., Company K, 18th Michigan Infantry
Russell, Jas., Company K, 18th Michigan Infantry
Shetteroe, Isadore, Company K, 18th Michigan Infantry
Stremp, Geo., Company K, 18th Michigan Infantry
Henks, T.W., Captain, 4th Missouri Cavalry
Brown, A.C., Company I, 2nd Ohio Infantry
Lewis, Lieutenant, 3rd Ohio Cavalry
Barnes, Wm., Company H, 22nd Ohio Infantry
Kearns, John, Company F, 40th Ohio Infantry
Oxley, Stewart, Company I, 51st Ohio Infantry
Gregory, W.W., Company C, 55th Ohio Infantry
Friesner, W.S., Company K, 58th Ohio Infantry
Boor, Wm., Private, Company D, 64th Ohio Infantry
Norris, Albert, Company A, 76th Ohio Infantry
Davis, J.W., Lieutenant, 77th Ohio Infantry
Yeisley, Wm., Company E, 102nd Ohio Infantry
Sheafer, I.N., Company E, 115th Ohio Infantry
Zazier, J.P., Company F, 115th Ohio Infantry
Morgan, L.G., Company D, 121st Ohio Infantry
Falderman, Benj., Company K, 121st Ohio Infantry
Fisher, Geo., Company K, 121st Ohio Infantry
Gaston, G.M., Company K, 121st Ohio Infantry
Green, Seth, Company K, 121st Ohio Infantry
Trent, Rob't A., Sergeant, Company B, 1st Tennessee Cavalry
Carver, Wm., Company B, 3rd Tennessee Cavalry
Hamilton, John, Company F, 3rd Tennessee Cavalry
Hamilton, R.N., Company F, 3rd Tennessee Cavalry
Hodges, Wiley J., Company F, 3rd Tennessee Cavalry
Jones, H.C., Corporal, Company F, 3rd Tennessee Cavalry
Atchley, P.L., Company K, 3rd Tennessee Cavalry
Pangle, Thos., Company K, 3rd Tennessee Cavalry
Elliott, J.W., Captain, Company F, 44th U.S.C.T.

After studying the multitude of names in this partial **Official Passengers List** which appeared in Chester D. Berry's *Loss of the Sultana and Reminiscences of Survivors* in 1892, one can only be amazed at what must have been an incredible overburdened load of passengers; and how many of them perished. It might be surprising to learn just how many of us may have had a relative upon her crowded decks. For military records, etc. (about *Sultana* passengers), contact the National Archives in Washington, D.C.

"Before daybreak the tramp of horses reminded us that our foragers were sallying forth. The red light from the countless camp-fires melted away as the dawn sole over the horizon, casting its wonderful gradations of light and color over the masses of sleeping soldiers, while the smoke of burning pine-knots befogged the chilly morning air. Then the bugles broke the impressive stillness, and the roll of drums was heard on all sides. Soon the scene was alive with blue coats and the hubbub of roll calling, cooking, and running for water to the nearest spring or stream. The surgeons looked to the sick and footsore, and weeded from the ambulances those who no longer needed to ride."*

Marching Through Georgia and the Carolinas,
By Daniel Oakey, Captain , 2nd Massachusetts Volunteers,
Battles and Leaders of the Civil War, The Century Co., 1887

Remember friends, as you pass by
As you are now so once was I
As I am now soon you must be
Prepare for death and follow me*

* Epitaph found on many tombstones

Index

A

B

C

132 **Index**

T

Taylor, R.G., 32, 38
Taylor, Tom, 24
Titanic, 2, 3, 4, 6, 42, 50, 51, 66

V

Vicksburg, 6, 20, 33, 35, 53, 56
Vindicator, 49

W

Washburn Commission, 52
Washington (hospital), 48
Webster, 48
White, George, 63
White, Manly C., 42
White Star Line, 2
Wilkie, Franc B., 10
Williams, George A., 33
Williams, Nathan S., 49
Wintringer, Nathan, 32
Wolverton, Horace May, 60, 61
Wolverton, James Thomas, 20, 40, 58, 59, 60, 61
Woolridge, Captain, 58
Wooldridge, William, 43

Y

Yeisley, Emanuel Hush, 56, 57
Young, George, 40

www.ingramcontent.com/pod-product-compliance
Lightning Source LLC
Chambersburg PA
CBHW060348090426
42734CB00011B/2068